DIAMONDS & PEBBLES

quotations

Eleanor Miller

Vesta Publications Limited
P.O. Box 1641
Cornwall, Ontario K6H 5V6
Canada

© Vesta Publications Limited, 1979

ISBN 0-919806 - 9 - 0

COVER DESIGN BY PETE MADSEN

ILLUSTRATIONS BY BRUCE COWAN AND FARRELL DUNHAM

Price $ 5.50

2

CONTENTS

REFLECTIONS

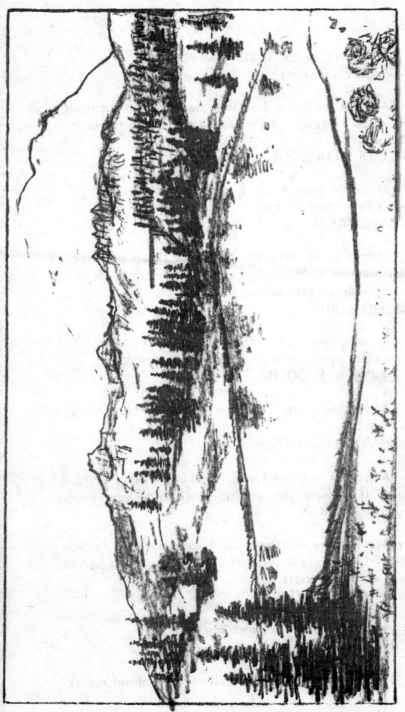

All fun is no fun at all.
—Dr. ERIKA FREEMAN

A vision without a task is a dream. A task without a vision is drudgery. A vision and a task are the hope of the world.
—CAROLYN DURHAM

All of us have bends in the road of life;
rarely do we come out even.
—DAVID WOLD

Always laugh when you can; it is cheap medicine. Merriment is a philosophy not well understood. It is the sunny side of existence.
—LORD BYRON

As machines get to be more and more like men,
men will come to be more and more like machines.
—JOSEPH W. KROOCH

A man has cause for regret only when he sows and no one reaps.
—CHARLES GOODYEAR

And think not you can guide the course of love, for love, if it finds you worthy, shall guide your course.
—KAHIL GIBRAN

Adversity is sometimes hard upon man; but for one man who can stand prosperity, there are a hundred that will stand adversity.
—THOMAS CARLYLE

A simple life is its own reward.
—GEORGE SANTAYANA

A lifetime is no time at all to comprehend the sky;

To entertain a sunset, snare twilight drifting by.
—BERTIE COLE BAYS

All that we are is the result of our thoughts.

A wise old owl sat on an oak;
The more he saw the less he spoke;
The less he spoke the more he heard;
Why aren't we like that wise old bird?
—EDWARD HERSEY RICHARDS

A happy life must be to a great extent a quiet life;
for it is only in an atmosphere of quiet that true joy
can live.
—BERTRAND RUSSELL

Act the part and you become the part.
—WILLIAM JAMES

A blizzard has a way of bringing people together.
—NORBERT SMITH

Always have a plan. To keep young, keep planning.
—GORDON P. MILLER
    (who planned a pear tree orchard at age 85)

A sharp tongue is the only edge tool that grows
keener with constant use.
—WASHINGTON IRVING

All things come round to him who will but wait.
—HENRY WADSWORTH LONGFELLOW

Art is a lie that enables us to realize the truth.
—PABLO PICASSO

A good book is the best of friends——the same today
and tomorrow.
—MARTIN TUPPER

Almost as bad as dying too soon, is living too long.
—HOWARD LUNDY

Ah! the clock is always slow; it is later than you think.
—ROBERT SERVICE

A fine quotation is a diamond on the finger of a man of wit——and a pebble in the hand of a fool.
—JOSEPH ROUX

A wise love values not so much the gift of the lover but the love of the giver.
—THOMAS A. KEMPIS

Art is like music——it should be enjoyed, not dissected.
—ERLE STANLEY GARDNER

Be silent always when you doubt your sense.
—ALEXANDER POPE

Being alone is a state of mind.
—JUDITH THOMPSON

Bad weather always looks much worse through a window.
—JOHN KIERAN

Be not simply good, but good for something.
—HENRY DAVID THOREAU

Before our breath is spent, before life's mill
grinds all too fine;
Let us this hour be still.
Let us take time——take time.

By all means use some time to be alone. Salute thyself!

See what thy soul doth wear.
—GEORGE HERBERT

Beware of despairing about yourself.
—ST. AUGUSTINE

Blood is thicker than water.
—SIR WALTER SCOTT

But I make this promise—to always stay surprised enough at life, to learn something new if I trip over it.
—HARRY REASONER

Bad roads are the best—for enjoying the scenery.

Be careful of the words you say; keep them soft and sweet. You never know from day to day—which ones you'll have to eat.

But words once spoken can never be recalled.
—WENTWORTH DILLON

Baboons and men have formed powerful working societies and have beaten the odds.

Complete possession is proved only by giving.
All which you are unable to give possesses you.
—ANDRE GIDE

Character is what you are in the dark.
—DWIGHT L. MOODY

Christmas is not just one day.

Charm is much more a matter of facial expression and voice rather than cosmetics and fashion.
—MARYA MANNES

Consider the source.

Clock-watchers! Time will pass .... Will you?

Curiosity is a characteristic of a vigorous mind.
—SAMUEL JOHNSON

Character is that which can do without success.
—RALPH WALDO EMERSON

Consider the old worn out clock.   Twice a day it is absolutely perfect.

Character is not born in a crisis; it is only revealed.

Don't worry about the future.
The present is all thou hast.
The future will soon be present.
And the present will soon be past.

Do not go gentle into that good night;
Old age should burn and rave at close of day;
Rage, rage against the dying of the light.
—DYLAN THOMAS

Dying is a necessary process to life.   From records of people who have been practically inside death's door, we do not need fear death—it is an experience of peace and tranquility.
—DR. LEWIS THOMAS

Do not push a friendship.   Don't rush.   Let the relationship grow in a natural way.
—EARL BLACKWELL

Do unto others as if you were others.

Do not worry; eat three square meals a day; say your
prayers; be courteous to your creditors;   keep your di-
gestion good; exercise;   go slow and go easy.
—ABRAHAM LINCOLN

Destiny is not a matter of chance.
It is a matter of choice.
—WILLIAM JENNINGS BRYAN

Don't tell me. Show me.

Defend me from my friends; I can defend myself from
my enemies.
—CLAUDE VILLARS

Delay is preferable to error.
—THOMAS JEFFERSON

Don't spend too much time dwelling on that castle
you're going to build some day. That little old house
that you're living in now may hold the most treasured
moments of your life.

Every noble work is at first impossible.
THOMAS CARLYLE

Enjoy your life without comparing it with that of others.
MARQUIS DE CONDORCET

Example is not the main thing in influencing others.
It is the only thing.
ALBERT SCHWEITZER

Everything in the world can be endured except continual prosperity.
—JOHANN VON GOETHE

11

Even very short periods of time add up to all the useful hours we need, if we plunge in to our work without delay.
—JOHN ERSKINE

Enjoy the sounds of silence.

Experience is what you get when you are looking for something else.

Each day is a gift.
—CHESTER D. ROBERTS

Experience is a wonderful thing. It enables you to recognize a mistake each time you repeat it.

Earth, that nourished thee, shall claim thy growth, to be resolved to earth again;   to mix forever with the elements;
To be a brother to the insensible rock,
The oak shall send his roots abroad,
and pierce thy mold.
—W. D. BRYANT

For every hill there is a valley.
For every plus there is a minus.
For every joy there is a disappointment.
This is life. A matter of ups and downs.
—JOHN WOODEN

For the East, and for the West
there is no salvation—
Except moral and religious regeneration.
—ALEXANDER SOLZHENITSYN

Fear not that thy life shall come to an end, but rather fear that it shall never have a beginning.
—CARDINAL NEWMAN

Far better it is to dare mighty things, to win glorious triumphs, even though checkered by failure—than to take rank with those poor spirits who neither enjoy much nor suffer much because they live in the gray twilight that knows not victory nor defeat.
—THEODORE ROOSEVELT

For every minute you are angry, you lose sixty seconds of happiness.
—RALPH WALDO EMERSON

Find your own true work, and you will find your heart's own.
Lose yourself in it and you will never think of sacrifices in its connection.

Greatness lies in dying at the right time.
—JOHN TYLER

Get in and bubble—the boiling water has all the fun.
—DR. JO STANCHFIELD

Great minds have purposes; others have wishes.
—WASHINGTON IRVING

Giving is receiving; receiving is giving.
That's really the secret
That lies behind living.

Good-byes are not important. It's what went before that counts.

—LUCILLE SCHOLLERMAN

Government is too big and important to be left to politicians.
—CHESTER BOWLES

Have a target and be your own man.
—Greg Edwards

Give a woman compliments instead of flowers. It pleases her more—and costs you less.

Good manners are the oil that keeps the gears of human contact from grinding.
—JENKIN LLOYD JONES

Great is the art of beginning, but greater the art of ending.

Many a poem is marred by a superfluous verse.
—HENRY WADSWORTH LONGFELLOW

Give me today and take tomorrow.

Happiness consists not in having many things—but in needing few.
—HENRY DAVID THOREAU

He may look like the devil, but the man may be a Saint.

How often we think it is important to be right whether we are or not.
—RAY LONGSTREET

Hold your thought on something you've always loved.
—JONATHAN LIVINGSTON SEAGULL

Happiness makes up in height for what it lacks in length.
—ROBERT FROST

How it improves people for us when we begin to love them.
—DAVID GRAYSON

14

We make more enemies by what we say than friends by what we do.

Human beings have always employed an enormous variety of clever devices for running away from themselves. We can keep ourselves so busy, stuff our heads with so much knowledge, involve ourselves with so many people, and cover so much ground, that we never have time to probe the wonderful world within.
—JOHN W. GARDNER

He who forgets the past is doomed to repeat it.
—EDDIE FISHER

How dull just to live in a permanent order of things, never expecting to face a challenge or overcome a problem. Such security does not really exist, you know.
—HELEN KELLER

Human life is unsafe at any speed—and therein lies much of its fascination.
—EDGAR ANSEL MOWRER

Habit is a cable; we weave a thread of it every day and at last we cannot break it.
—HORACE MANN

Health—wealth—happiness—and enough time to enjoy all three.

It's honest work. It is much less of a hassle than working in a bank or office. There are no problems with dress, and it's certainly no more mindless than being a file clerk, or something.
—CAROL ROBERTS
(a former doctoral candidate in linguistics at Harvard, working as a cleaning lady)

I am not young enough to know everything.
—JAMES BARRIE

I praise loudly. I blame softly.
—CATHERINE THE GREAT, OF RUSSIA

If you like it, I like it.
—JACK SHORE

I had a sparrow alight on my shoulder for a moment
while I was hoeing in my garden, and I felt more dis-
tinguished by that circumstance than I should have been
by any epaulet I could have worn.
—HENRY DAVID THOREAU

If a nation will not help the vast majority of people
who are poor, how can it save the few people who are rich?
—JOHN KENNEDY

I believe in getting outside my box by changing
rhythm, space and time. To follow one lifestyle in one
place would be to ignore the rest of the world.
—MARY LONGLAND

In youth, we run into difficulties. In old age, difficulties run into us.
—JOSH BILLINGS

I like this lifestyle. It is simple. I eat fruits and
vegetables I grow myself. No meat. I eat when I'm
hungry and I go to bed when I'm sleepy.
—GEORGE MORIKAMI
(89 year old millionaire, who spends his days toiling as a
pineapple farmer)

I sighed because the day was dark—

16

and then I met a child who had no eyes.

I complained because I had no shoes—
Until I met a man who had no feet.

It takes a long time to become young.
– PABLO PICASSO   (at age 86)

It is a known fact that we do find time to do the things
we really want to do.
–ANNE LINDBERGH

If you keep busy, enjoy your work, and take pride in
it, you will stay young.
–MARY VESPILLE
(82 year old woman doing it alone on a ranch)

I wish I were where I was when I wanted to be where
I am now.
–JAMES T. STAINBACK, JR.

If you want to be happy and healthy, do one of the
basic things in life—sing! Sing in the shower, in the
car, on the trail; let off steam, and sing!

It isn't the stress—it's the way you take it.
–Dr. HANS SELYE

In this life, no one is completely free. We are all tied
to someone, or something, or some place. If not one of
these—then to our conscience.

I'm too old to cry, and it hurts too much to laugh.
–ABRAHAM LINCOLN

I don't believe in age. It's the way you look at

things, as though you were looking at them for the first time. A curiosity about everything around. Age is relative to one's appetite for life.
—MARTHA GRAHAM
(at 81, toured Bangkok with her Dance Company)

Injustice anywhere is a threat to justice everywhere.
—MARTIN LUTHER KING, JR.

I believe in the sun even when it doesn't shine.

Imitation is the sincerest of flattery.
—C. C. COLTON

It is wise to keep in mind that neither success nor failure is ever final.
—ROGER BABSON

I cannot close the door upon a friend, but when my guests have gone, and I'm alone—how really fond of solitude I've grown!
—LAURENCE E. ESTES

It is easier to stay out than to get out.
—MARK TWAIN

It is impossible to enjoy idling thoroughly, unless one has plenty of work to do.
—JEROME K. JEROME

I have spent many a day alone, but never a lonely day.
—BILLY GRAHAM

I will not follow where the path may lead, but I will go where there is no path, and I will leave a trail.
—MURIEL STRODE

18

I owe all my success in life to having been always a
quarter of an hour beforehand.
–LORD NELSON

I have two doctors: my left leg and my right.
–GEORGE M. TREVELYAN

I went to the woods because I wished to live deliberately–
to front only the essential facts of life and see if I could
not learn what it had to teach, and not, when I came to die,
discover that I had not lived.
–HENRY DAVID THOREAU

It is useless to send armies against ideas.
–GEORG BRANDES

I have never had a complex about growing old.
–ELSA LANCHESTER

If there's no chance of failure, how can anyone hope
for success?
–RUSSELL KIRK

It's the truth that hurts.

If the day is dark and gloomy, I pack even more enthusiasm into it. Actually, I like a dark day occasionally.
–NORMAN VINCENT PEALE

In the laboratory we learn more by what goes wrong
than by what goes right.
–DR. PAT SMITH

I discovered the secret of the sea in meditation upon
a dewdrop.
–KAHIL GIBRAN

I have four things to live by:
1. Don't say nothing that will hurt anybody.
2. Don't give advice.
3. Don't complain.
4. Don't explain.
—DEATH VALLEY SCOTTY

It is better to spell love incorrectly than to spell hate correctly.

In every man's life there are pin—points of time that govern his destiny.
—WILLARD MOTLEY

I do my thing and you do yours. I am not in your world to live up to your expectations. And you are not in the world to live up to mine.

If you live like you're poor, you're poor.
And if you live like you're rich, you're rich.
—JUDY NORD

In Cicero's time, if people had bread and circus games, they were happy. Today, if they have beer, snacks, and the tube, they are happy.

If you take credit for the rain, you've also got to take credit for the drought.
—HUBERT HUMPHREY

If you have candles on the table, light them.
—GROUCHO MARX

If you must take a side in a family argument, choose the outside.

I have studied my animals, and I see in them the most loyalty, the most joy, the most purity, the most everything.
—DORIS DAY

If you don't say anything, you don't have to deny it.
—CALVIN COOLIDGE

I keep my answers small and keep them near. Small answers, hearth—hugging thoughts are a bulwark against fear.
—ELIZABETH JENNINGS

I made the wrong mistakes.
—YOGI BERRA

I hold that a little rebellion is a good thing——and is as neccessary in the political world as a storm is in the physical world.
—THOMAS JEFFERSON

It's only a coincidence, but it's interesting to note that man's best friend can't talk.
—LANE OLINGHOUSE

It's a wonderful experience to be living in a time of change. Change brings stress, but stress produces strength.
—Dr. DIXIE LEE RAY

If it doesn't hurt, you are not doing it right.
—BALLERINA TO APPRENTICE

If you would have success, bring your tools with you. And be willing to spend a part of each day keeping them sharpened.
—BOB ROBERTSON

It requires greater virtues to support good fortune than bad.
—LA ROCHEFOUCAULD

I learned to work mornings, when I could skim the cream off the day, and use the rest for cheese—making.
—JOHANN VON GOETHE

I had a friend.
—CHARLES KINGSLEY
(responding to the question of the secret of his successful life)

It isn't what you do, dear, but what you have left undone,
That gives you a bit of a heart—ache,
At the setting of the sun.

It is better to live rich than to die rich.
—SAMUEL JOHNSON

I will study and prepare myself,
Then some day my time will come.
—ABRAHAM LINCOLN

I have often regretted my speech, never silence.
—MAXIM   (1060)

If physicke fayle for the advayle,
Three Doctors shall you find,
Doctor due diet,
And Doctor quiet,
And Doctor merry-mynde.

If you can't solve your problem, change your problem.
—HUGH DOWNS

22

Keep your face always turned toward the sunshine
...and the shadows will fall behind you.
—WALT WHITMAN

Look well to this day. Yesterday is but a dream;
tomorrow is only a vision. Look well, therefore, to this
day.

Let us be of good cheer, remembering that the misfortunes hardest to bear are those that never come.
—JAMES RUSSELL LOWELL

Look for a lovely thing and you will find it.
It is not far—it never will be far.
—SARA TEASDALE

Life can only be understood backwards;
but it must be lived forwards.
—STOREN KIERKEGAARD

Let us take time to know the thoughts of men;
Time to know beauty; time to feel again calm and con—
tent of soul———
The quiet power of meditation through a gentle hour.
—WINONA EVANS REEVES

Life is not the end — it is the road.
—GERTRUDE HANSEN

Let the love in your life shine on like the moon and
the stars and the sun. Love stays alive just as long as
you can grow with it. Come to life! Come to life! We
can make a party out of living!
—PAMELA

Love makes one more calm about many things, so
one is more fit for one's work.
—VINCENT VAN GOGH

Look, listen, live.
Life speaks a varied language.

Life without the possibility of success would be boring; and there can be no possibility of success unless the possibility of failure also exists.
—RUSSELL KIRK

Luck is the thing that happens when the proper preparation meets the right opportunity.

Let discontent alone, and she will shut her mouth and let you sing.
—JAMES WHITCOMB RILEY

Life is but love of simple things like these:
A shelf of friendly books that call, no other faintest sound.
—BLANCHE WALTRIP ROSE

Let us take time for the book, the song, the golden weather made for the happiness of friends together.

Let sleeping dogs lie.
—CHARLES DICKENS

Let your boat of life be light——packed with only what you need: a homesy home and simple pleasures: one or two friends, worth the name, someone to love and someone to love you;   a cat, a dog, a pipe or two, enough to drink——for thirst is a dangerous thing.
—JEROME K. JEROME

Life is short; live it up.
—NIKITA KHRUSCHEV

Little I ask; my wants are few,
I only wish a hut of stone,
(A very plain brownstone will do)
That I may call my own.
—OLIVER WENDELL HOLMES

Love is getting happiness out of another person's
happiness.
—W. W. BROADBENT

Make the day count. Pack your cares into as little
compass as convenience allows.
—ROBERT SOUTHEY

Much of the world's work is done by people who
don't feel very well.
—FLOYD MILLER
(thinking of Charles P. Steinmetz)

Make yourself necessary to somebody.
—RALPH WALDO EMERSON

More is not always better.

My motto as I live and learn is
Dig, and be dug in return.
—LANGSTON HUGHES

May happy times decorate your holiday season———
May lovely memories sustain you in the New Year——
May the wonder of Christmas be with you forever.

Make the most of yourself, for that is all there is of you.
—RALPH WALDO EMERSON

My house, my house, though thou are small,

Thou art to me the Escurial.
—GEORGE HERBERT

Man may mar the earth, but nature covers over——
With the falling snow, with the swinging clover.
—KATHRYN MCCAY

Miracles sometimes occur, but one has to work terribly hard for them.
—CHAIM WEIZMANN

Music is the universal language of mankind.
—HENRY WADSWORTH LONGFELLOW

Nature and books belong to the eyes that see them.
—RALPH WALDO EMERSON

No bird soars too high if he soars with his own wings.
—WILLIAM BLAKE

Nothing is really work unless you'd rather be doing something else.
—JAMES M. BARRIE

No night should fall but that a man's conscious should wrestle with the mistakes of the day, and made corrections for the next day.
—POPE PAUL

Nature always has the effect of lifting the spirit; not just on a sunny day, but in all kinds of weather, if you get in tune with her.
—NORMAN VINCENT PEALE

Not——where can I go for help?
But, where can I go with help?
—HUGH DOWNS

Nothing is so good as it seems beforehand.
—GEORGE ELIOT

None knows the weight of another's burden.
—GEORGE HUBERT

No matter how fair the sun shines, still, it must set.
—RAIMUND

Necessity makes even the timid brave.
—SALLUST

Nothing can bring you peace but yourself.
—RALPH WALDO EMERSON

No question is ever settled until it is settled right.
—ELLA WHEELER WILCOX

No race can prosper until it learns that there is as
much dignity in tilling a field as in writing a poem.
—BOOKER T. WASHINGTON

Nothing in this world is so powerful as an idea whose
time has come .
—VICTOR HUGO

No man manages his affairs as well as a tree does.
—GEORGE BERNARD SHAW

Nothing so needs reforming as other people's habits.
—MARK TWAIN

One may live as a conqueror, king, or a magistrate,
but he must die as a man.
—DANIEL WEBSTER

Our whole social life is in essence but a long, slow striving for the victory of justice over force.
—JOHN GALSWORTHY

Often to be most eloquent is to be silent.

Our chief want in life is somebody who shall make us do what we can.
—RALPH WALDO EMERSON

One can never tell just what the result of one's actions will be; for with every deed he is sowing a seed, though its harvest he may never see.

Opportunity doesn't drop in unexpectedly; it has to be invited.
—LEO H. DARROW

One boy is a boy.
Two boys are half a boy.
And three boys are no boy at all.
(often quoted to Charles Lindbergh by his father)

One of the lessons of history is that nothing is often a good thing to do and always a clever thing to say.
—WILL DURANT

One motivation is worth ten threats, two pressures, and six reminders.
—PAUL SWEENEY

One of the virtues of being young is that you don't let the facts get in the way of your imagination.
—SAM LEVENSON

One never knows where simple little things will lead

you.
—MARJORIE REYNOLDS

One machine can replace one hundred ordinary men, but no machine can replace one extra—ordinary man.
—JOHN CHANCELLOR

One half of the world cannot understand the pleasures of the other half.
—JANE AUSTEN

Pleasure is very seldom found where it is sought.
—SAMUEL JOHNSON

Praise is a device for making a man deserve it.
—FRANKLIN P. JONES

Poise is the ability to be ill at ease inconspicuously.

Put yourself in good spirits and enjoy the day.
—NORMAN VINCENT PEALE

Reading is sometimes an ingenious device for avoiding thought.
—SIR ARTHUR HELPS

Remember that happiness is everyday living. Eating. Breathing. Seeing. Relating. Loving. Talking. Listening. Walking. . . . . These are all things that make life beautiful.
—THEODORE I. RUBIN

Real friendship is slow of growth.

Recollection is the only paradise here on earth from which we cannot be turned out.
—JOHANN RICHTER

Rise with the lark, and with the lark to bed.
—HURDIS

Rest is a good thing——but boredom is its brother.
—FRANCOIS VOLTAIRE

Right is right——but there are many kinds of wrongs.
—FRANKIE AVALON

Solitude is one essential means of achieving a balance amidst life's distractions. . .
This is difficult because the world does not understand
the need to be alone.
—ANNE LINDBERGH

Striving to better, oft we mar what was well.
—WILLIAM SHAKESPEARE

Sound has no meaning except in relation to silence.
—PATRICIA I. OUGHTON

Suddenly it dawned on me——I didn't want the things
the others kids had——I wanted my own. There's a difference.
—FLIP WILSON

Speech is the index of the mind.
—SENECA

Success is getting what you want; happiness is
wanting what you get.

Smells, like music have that power to evoke the past.
A good strong whiff can stab you to the heart with pain
and longing and remembrance. More and more we are becoming a deodorized nation. They've been taking away

the God—intended smells we used to have.
—JOHN CROSBY

Self—conquest is the greatest of victories.
—PLATO

Sometimes they'll give a war and nobody will come.
—CARL SANDBURG

Suffering overcomes the mind's inertia, develops the thinking powers, opens up a new world, and drives the soul to action.
—ANTHONY H. EVANS

The great art to learn much is to undertake a little at a time.
—JOHN LOCKE

To have what we want is riches; but to be able to do without is power.
—GEORGE MACDONALD

The men who try to do something and fail are better than those who try to do nothing and succeed.
—LLOYD JONES

Turn every defeat into a victory.

There is no grief which time does not soften.
—CICERO

To love is to stop comparing.
—BERNARD GRASSET

This I learned from the shadow of a tree;
Our influence may fall where we may never be.

31

The most difficult thing in life is to know yourself.
—THALES

There is nothing harder than the softness of indif—
ference.
—JUAN MONTALVO

Trust is just holding on to one finger.
—PATRICIA D. PACE

Times are changed with him who marries; there are
no more bypath meadows, where you may innocently
linger——but the road lies long and straight and dusty
to the grave.
—ROBERT LOUIS STEVENSON

The ceiling is unlimited.

The more success you have, the harder it gets.
—GEORGE C. SCOTT

Treat people as if they were what they ought to be.
Then you help them become what they ought to become.
—JOHANN VON GOETHE

The highest and most lofty trees have the most
reason to dread the thunder.
—CHARLES ROLLIN

Three things you must have to keep mentally healthy:
A task.. A plan... and freedom.
—JOHN TYLER

The work will wait while you show the child the

rainbow, but the rainbow won't wait while you do the work.
—PATRICIA CLAFFORD

The man who only hopes is hopeless.

Two things fill the mind with ever increasing wonder and awe; the starry Heavens above me and the moral law within me.
—IMMANUEL KANT

The sun will not rise, or set, without my notice, and thanks.
—WINSLOW HOMER

'Tis more brave to live than to die.
—MEREDITH

Take time to deliberate; but when the time for action arrives, stop thinking and go in.
—ANDREW JACKSON

The strongest man upon earth is he who stands alone.
—HENRIK IBSEN

There is always something to worry you. It comes as regularly as the sunrise.
—BENJAMIN DISRAELI

Truth exists; only falsehood has to be invented.
—GEORGES BRAZUE

There is too much emphasis on fun——the fun of trying things for temporarily induced pleasure. Real pleasures is something you feel in your gut. It comes from participation and accomplishment.
—Dr. ERIKA FREEMAN

33

There is a difference between hearing and listening. You can hear words, but you have to listen for thoughts.
—TANNER

There is no good substitute for wisdom, but silence is the best that has yet been discovered.
—H. W. SHAW

The trouble with winning is that you've got to keep on doing it.
—GERALD FORD

The remarkable thing is not that it is done well——but that it is done at all.   (Like a dog walking on his hind legs).

To be quoted is a mark of importance; to be misquoted is a mark of great importance.
—SYDNEY J. HARRIS

The only way to have a thing forever is to give it away.
—OSCAR WILDE

The Mona Lisa was not painted by a committee.
—TOM MUSICK

There is only one success——
to be able to spend your life in your own way.
—CHRISTOPHER MORLEY

There are two reasons for doing anything——
a good reason, and the real reason.
—J. P. MORGAN

The height of folly is to live poor so you can die rich.

The more we are able to see, the more we look for.
—SAUL BASS

To live in the hearts we leave behind is not to die.
—THOMAS CAMPBELL

The greatest happiness you can have is knowing that you do not necessarily require happiness.
—WILLIAM SAROYAN

To be 70 years young is sometimes more hopeful than to be 40 years old.
—OLIVER WENDELL HOLMES

Today's burden can be endured. It is tomorrow's burden that is more than a man can bear.

The greater the difficulty, the greater the glory.
—CICERO

Time goes, you say? Ah, no. Alas, time stays; we go.
—HENRY DOBSON

To die will be an awfully big adventure.
—JAMES M. BARRIE

This is my last message to you,
In sorrow seek happiness.
—FEODOR DOSTOEVSKY

The happiest of all lives is a busy solitude.
—VOLTAIRE

To play great music, you must keep your eye on a

distant star.
—YEHUDI MENUHIN

The important news this week is not what has hap—
pened——it's what hasn't happened.
—NEIL MACNEIL

The secret of happiness is to learn to live within
one's limitations, whether they be physical, financial,
or circumstantial.
—MARY HINTON

Tomorrow is going to be better. Just compare a tulip
bulb with a tulip.
—Dr. MARC CATHY

The first principle of intelligent tinkering is to save
all the pieces.
—ALDO LEOPOLD

Use what language you will, you can never say any—
thing but what you are.
—RALPH WALDO EMERSON

With fun alone there is nothing to turn to but more
fun. It's like pulling a rubber band over and over—you
lose your stretch.
—DR. ERIKA FREEMAN

Wisdom is ofttimes nearer when we stoop than when we soar.
—WILLIAM WORDSWORTH

What we see depends mainly on what we look for.
—JOHN LUBBOCK

We are for the most part more lonely when we go

abroad than when we stay in our chambers. A man thinking
or working is always alone; let him be where he will.
—HENRY DAVID THOREAU

We need periods of aloneness; from them we generate
the physical and spiritual reinvigoration for our more crowded days.
—BILLY GRAHAM

We were ecumenical before Pope John; integrated
before civil rights; international before the United Na-
tions; we had a conservation program before Lady Bird;
sang folksongs before Peter, Paul and Mary; were taking
mind—expanding trips before LSD; we had volunteers
serving this country before the Peace Corps and Vista.
And we started Women's Liberation.
We are the Girl Scouts.

We read the stories, and the child in all of us laughed for
joy because Hans Christian Anderson took the broken
things in life, the discarded, the sad, the unwanted,
———and wove them into magic.

Wisdom does not lie in knowing what to do ultimately——
but in what to do next.
—HERBERT HOOVER

Whenever I prepare for a journey, I prepare as though
for death. Should I never return, all is in order. This is
what life has taught me.
—KATHERINE MANSFIELD

Wisdom is knowing when you can't be wise.
—PAUL ENGLE

When it is dark enough, you can see the stars.
—CHARLES A. BEARD

Weep not that the world changes—did it keep a stable, changeless state, 'twere cause indeed to weep.
—WILLIAM CULLEN BRYANT

We must change to master change.
—LYNDON B. JOHNSON

Wanting is more fun than having.
—DOROTHY WILAN

Wear the old coat and buy the new book.
—AUSTIN PHELPS

We see things not as they are but as we are.
—IMMANUEL KANT

What one has to do, usually can be done.
—ELEANOR ROOSEVELT

We are all under the tyranny of time.
—FRANK REYNOLDS

We exaggerate misfortune and happiness alike. We are never either so wretched or so happy as we say we are.
—BALZAC

When you get up close you find nothing is perfect.

Your tastes determine your destiny.

You can never tell what you'll meet when you're out without your gun.
—CLARISSA HANSEN

The grand show is eternal. It is always sunrise somewhere.
The dew is never all dried at once; a shower is forever falling, vapor is ever rising; eternal sunrise, eternal sunset, eternal dawn.
—JOHN MUIR

The time to be happy is now.
The place to be happy is here.
The way to be happy is to make others so.
—ROBERT INGERSOLL

Tomorrow exists only in the mind as an image of what may be. Yesterday exists only in the mind as memory of what has been. But today is ours!
—HAROLD BLAKE WALKER

Watching a peaceful death of a human being reminds us of a falling star; one of the million lights in a vast sky that flares up for a brief moment, only to disappear into the endless   night forever. . . . .
—ELISABETH KUBLER—ROSS

When a person dies, he's neither down in the ground or up in the sky; he's living in the hearts and eyes of people he encountered along the way.
—JOHN STEINBECK

What do you mean by saying you are bored, man?
Engarde, sire! The waiting world still invites you to a duel!
—HAL BOYLE

PEOPLE

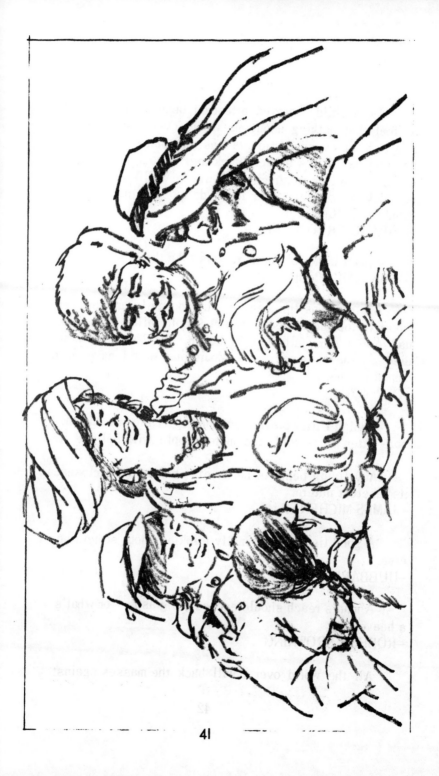

As a child I craved attention because I was made to feel that nothing about me would ever attract attention or bring me admiration. I was told that I would never have beaux; I was an ugly duckling. I couldn't dance or skate as well as other girls. I was a wallflower. Then one day a boy asked me for a date. His name was Franklin D. Roosevelt.
–ELEANOR ROOSEVELT

A man is not old until regrets take the place of dreams.
–JOHN BARRYMORE

As tragic as the men who die too early are the men who live too long. Had Benedict Arnold fallen at Saratoga, had Aaron Burr fallen at Yorktown, had Marshal Petain died on the Marne. . . .   Mountains would have been named for them.
–G. P. JONES

Adolph Hitler proved that the bigger the lie, and the more often it is told, the more people will believe it.

Any living being is better off when it lives closest to its inherent nature.
–JAMES MICHENER

A good listener is usually thinking about something else.
–HUBBARD

A man's reach should exceed his grasp,   or what's a heaven for.
–ROBERT BROWNING

All the world over I will back the masses against

against the classes.
—WILLIAM GLADSTONE

A dying man needs to die, as a sleepy man needs to sleep.
—STEWART ALSOP

As we grow old, the beauty steals inward.
—RALPH WALDO EMERSON

A really busy person never knows how much he weighs.
—EDGAR WATSON HOWE

A person is a variety of things.

American women wouldn't be so keen on liberation if they could see the role of the women of Russia.
—TOM MONTGOMERY

A successful man is one who can lay a firm foundation with the bricks that others throw at him.
—DAVID BRINKLEY

An old woman is as tough as a boiled owl.
—EDNA MILLER

All too often we adults work so hard at our fun that we really don't have fun at all.
—EDA J. LESHAN

A politician must always remember that his past is before him.
—GENE SHALIT

Accomplishments are performed by two types of

people—those who are smart and know the job can be done, and those who are dumb, and don't know the job can't be done.

A hungry man is not a free man.
—ADLAI STEVENSON

All people smile in the same language.

A man who has nothing to hide never hides anything.
—SAM ERVIN

Art is I. Science is we.
—Dr. JAMES SALK

A good man possesses a kingdom.
—THYESTES

Ah, you flavor everything; you are the vanilla of society.
—SYDNEY SMITH

A good listener is not only popular, but after awhile he knows something.
—WILSON MIZNER

Anybody is as their land and air is.
—GERTRUDE STEIN

A person who does not understand another's silence will not understand his words.

As long as the bosses pretend they are paying us a decent wage we will pretend that we are working.
—SOVIET WORKER'S SAYING

A man is what he thinks about all day long.
—RALPH WALDO EMERSON

Ah, people dressed for the theatre in those days.
Nobody does anymore——they might as well stay in their
sleeping clothes.
—GLORIA SWANSON

A hero is no braver than an ordinary man, but he is
brave five minutes longer.
—RALPH WALDO EMERSON

A man is not old as long as he is seeking something.
—JEAN ROSTAND

Be to yourself as you would to your friends.
—WILLIAM SHAKESPEARE

Back of serenity there is self—discipline. No one
speaks with authority to others who has not first spoken
with authority to himself.

Be odd or eccentric if you choose. Nobody else really
cares, you know.
—THOMAS COLLINS

————But he's awfully good with his hands.
(said about Sir Isaac Newton in his early school years)

Better to trust a man who is frequently in error, than a
man who is never in doubt.
—ERIC SEVAREID

Bloom where you are planted.

Barbara Walters? Well, to work with, she's just a piece

45

of cake.
–DOUGLAS KIKER

Bores are people who are bored.

Better keep yourself clean and bright; you are the window through which you must see the world.
–GEORGE BERNARD SHAW

Best be yourself, imperial, plain, and true.
–ROBERT BROWNING

But everyone is so old!
––94 year old woman entering a nursing home

Be still–and listen to all persons; even the dull and silent have their story to tell.

Be attractive if you can. If you can't manage that, look distinctive, eccentric, sexy, memorable, but not unkempt.

––I rushed to the mirror and picked two possibilities for myself––
–MARY MANNES

Being the wife of the prime minister is not the gla–morous, exciting life most people think it is. It's not a free life–but it's a good one.
–MARGARET TRUDEAU

Be willing to fail temporarily––but pick yourself up and return to the fight.
–NORMAN VINCENT PEALE

Creative people never stop; they are always on the

46

front line of something.
—Dr. ERIKA FREEMAN

Curiosity has kept me from ever being bored.
—GLORIA SWANSON

Dad, get off my back, and get on my side.
—RICHARD ROBERTS

Don't pay any attention to honkers.
—DOUG MILLER

Doyle grew so tired of the detective Sherlock Holmes that he prematurely killed him, and was forced to bring him back to life by his readers.
—SYDNEY J. HARRIS

Don't put too much icin' to my cake. Never did go much fer icin'.
—MINNIE BROOKS
(on her 100th birthday)

Don't muddle in the middle. If you are cozily set—tled in the middle years of life, quit being so cozy and do something!   Don't be afraid to continue the learning adventures that have brought you this far.

Dear Marian Anderson, because of you, I am.
—LEONTYNE PRICE

Everyone needs beauty as well as bread.
—JOHN MUIR

Every man desires to live long, but no man would be old.
—JONATHAN SWIFT

Each person must have elbow room and opportunity for occasional solitude.
—MARYA MANNES

Everything comes to him who hustles while he waits.
—THOMAS EDISON

Every hero becomes a bore at last.
—RALPH WALDO EMERSON

Even though my visiting her doesn't make her any better, in some way I like to think that it makes me better.
—ELIZABETH NYBERG

Everyone should have a field of expertise.

Every good athlete has got to have a lot of little boy in him, as well as a lot of man:
—JOE GARAGIOLA

Eventually we will all run out of time.
Look to this day!

Everybody is ignorant, only along different lines.
—WILL ROGERS

Everyone is too old for something,
But no one is too old for everything.

Every man meets his Waterloo at last.
—WENDELL PHILLIPS

Everyone needs a warm personal enemy or two to keep him free of rust in the movable parts of his mind.
—GENE FOWLER

Every man should be able to do something all by himself; something that gives him a sense of mastery; fly, sing, write, bake a loaf of bread, handle a Bowie knife, tap dance, find a new star, carve in ivory. Man needs to solo.
–BRUCE GOULD

Friendship is almost always the union of a part of mind with a part of another; people are friends in spots.
–GEORGE SANTAYANA

Franklin Delano Roosevelt was 90% Eleanor and 10% mush.
–ALICE ROOSEVELT LONGWORTH

For my part, I travel not to go anywhere, but to go. I travel for travel's sake. The great affair is to move.
–ROBERT LOUIS STEVENSON

For most of us, such a day would have been one of the most hectic of our lives. But for the Queen of England, it was almost a holiday.
–GILLIAN FRANKS
    (describing a quiet day for Queen Elizabeth––)
(She held an investiture for 176 people, had an official lunch, received two diplomats, saw her dressmaker,   had a   thirty minute talk with the prime minister, and went out to a state dinner)

Grandmothers don't have to do anything. They just have to be there.
–ERIC ANDERSON

Go out tomorrow, looking for people to like. You'll find them everywhere. And doing this will make you

happy, and I mean really happy.
—NORMAN VINCENT PEALE

Great eaters and great sleepers are incapable of any—
thing else that is great.
—KING HENRY IV

Give yourself a kiss.
—DR. IRENE KASSORLA

Growing up is the hardest thing you have to do.
—CHARLTON HESTON

He built roads all over Africa, but he never thought
to fix up the road to our hill country farmhouse.
—MRS. BENITO MUSSOLINI

He who has a thousand friends has not a friend to
spare. And he who has one enemy shall meet him
everywhere.
—RALPH WALDO EMERSON

How do you live to be 100? Very simple. Get a
chronic disease. Then you'll be forced to take excellent care of yourself.
—PAUL BAYLESS

He was death on banks——no getting around it. But
there was goodness, too.
—LOLA PARKER BETENSON
   (sister of Butch Cassidy)

He's the only sweetheart I ever had.
—BESS TRUMAN

He walked straight, talked straight, and never forgot

50

the place where he came from.
—MARY DOWELL
(friend of Harry Truman)

Have more than thou showest,
Speak less than thou knowest,
Lend less than thou owest.
—WILLIAM SHAKESPEARE

He was 39.
(Last line in a Los Angeles Times obituary column
    reporting Jack Benny's death)

He wasn't the greatest thinker of his time, nor the greatest statesman, but he was the greatest man.
—ERIC SEVAREID
    (speaking of George Washington)

He was fresh and full of faith that something would turn up.
—BENJAMIN DISRAELI

He seems to have seen better days, as who has not who has seen yesterday?
—LORD BYRON

He didn't give me my first movie kiss——
but it's the first one I remember.
—OLIVIA DE HAVILLAND——speaking of Errol Flynn

He let me walk with greatness.
—ANDY WILLIAMS
(speaking of Robert Kennedy)

Harry, I hope you left a box of aspirin in your desk drawer for me.
—GERALD FORD   (on assuming the presidency)

51

He is very direct in his remarks. He will look you in the eye, and tell you what he thinks about you, or someone else.
—EUGENIA KULIKOV
    (speaking of Alexander Solzhenitsyn)

He sticks pretty close to the Constitution and his wife——and he's married to both of them.
—MIKE MANSFIELD
(speaking of Senator Sam Ervin)

History will tell us;
Greeks were famous for liberty;
Romans were famous for law;
Britains were famous for parliamentary government;
Americans are famous for educating the masses.

He has no friend who has many friends.
—ARISTOTLE

I think this is the most extraordinary collection of talent, of human knowledge, that has ever been gathered together at the White House, with the possible exception of when Thomas Jefferson dined alone.
—JOHN FITZGERALD KENNEDY
(address at White House honoring Nobel Prize Winners——
        April 1962)

I just love 'em like brothers, I don't try to give a sermon. I just like to think I can help them forget their troubles for an hour or two.
—JUDY LYNN
(singing at a Federal Penitentiary)

If you manage to live to 65, you have a good chance for ten more years.

I remember my old man. People would have called him a common man. But he didn't consider himself so. First he was a street car conductor——then a farmer. He owned the poorest lemon farm in California. He sold it——before oil was discovered on the land.
—RICHARD M. NIXON

I am inspired by the Indians' relationship to the land. They have a well thought out way of living in harmony with nature. We're all asking how to cope with nature today, and it seems to me the Indians had a few of the answers.
—T. C. MCLUHAN

I become discouraged about mankind when I read the newspaper; I become encouraged when I see him in the laboratory.
—Dr. S. STANLEY SMITH

I never got married because I like to sit by the window.

I hope that you will find joy in this day, and that you will be a part of someone else finding joy in theirs.

In order to be a realist you must believe in miracles.
—DAVID BEN—GURION

I have always been grateful for my deafness, for it made it possible for me to live in a world of my own with—out listening to babble.
—THOMAS EDISON

I have suffered from being misunderstood, but I would have suffered a hell of a lot more if I had been

understood.
—CLARENCE DARROW

It takes a mess of people to help me do it alone.
—PAUL HARVEY

It is impossible for an author or a newscaster to be completely objective. Even Cronkite can slant a story by a raise of the eyebrow or a twist of the mouth.

If all the heads of state in the world today were in a chamber music group, there would be no problems. There, the give and take is perfect.
—Dr. EUGENE GREENFIELD

It is not how old you have grown, but how you have grown old.

I care not so much, what I am in the opinion of others, as what I am in my own.
—MICHAEL DE MONTAIGNE

It is never too late to be what you might have been
—GEORGE ELIOT

I was never in a hurry in my life.
—SHIRALI MISLIMOV
(the oldest man in the world when he died at 168)

I have learned a good deal from my own talks.
—THOMAS C. HALLIBURTON

I don't play a musical instrument; I don't drive a car; I don't play bridge; I don't dance——don't do much

of anything, really. But I'm a wife, a mother, a grand—
mother, and I'm happy I am what I am.
—LEILA TRIPP

If I had my life to live over, I would have made a
rule to read some poetry and listen to some music at least
once a week; for perhaps the parts of my brain now atro—
phied would thus have been kept active through use.
—CHARLES DARWIN

I've never met a man who didn't know a lot more
about some one thing than I did.
—ABRAHAM LINCOLN

If he had to live his life over again, he wouldn't
have time.
(SAID OF BOB HOPE)

I love playing grandfather roles. I don't have to worry
about a hair piece. or bags under my eyes. I can just be
myself. and it's fun.
—RAY MILLAND

I fell short of my goal. All my life my dream was to
to be speaker of the house.
—GERALD FORD

In order to learn how to be a good soccer player, I
studied mathematics and chess.
—PELE

Indians had profound respect for the great Spirit who
was not a deity as much as a principle that set the stars
in the sky and brought the seasons in perfect rhythm.
—FREDDA DUDLEY BALLING

If I become free, you become free.
—MARTIN LUTHER KING

I appear on the stage just as I do on the street. And that't the way I appear on the television. The make—up people try to make you look younger and more attractive than you are. I'd rather be myself.
—ELSA LANCHESTER

I would give up all my genius, and all my books, if there were only some woman, somewhere, who cared whether or not I came home late for dinner.
—IVAN TURGENEV

It is as easy for the strong man to be strong as the weak to be weak.
—RALPH WALDO EMERSON

I'm so full of music, if I don't sit down and let if flow out, I think I would burst from the pressure.
—RUDOLPH FRIML

I developed my sense of rhythm by beating with spoons on pots and pans as a child, on a tenement floor.
—LIONEL HAMPTON

I feel I've been a fortunate man because I've had the privilege of being poor. I simply had to work and I had a chance to learn day by day.
—LAWRENCE WELK

If you want to get high——meditate.
—GOVERNOR JERRY BROWN

I think laughing and goofing off are just as important as the serious things in life. Being famous and all that

is not so great. After all, we actually go after fame and
fortune so we can goof off.
—ROBERT REDFORD

Is love possible? For me, it is. Every man knows
that for himself.
—ERNEST HEMINGWAY

I can't say I love, you Tchaikovsky, when I have to
play your Concerto sixteen times in a month.
—VAN CLIBURN

I cannot make you happy unless I know what makes
you unhappy.
—LOIS WYSE

I don't want anybody to forget Babe Ruth. I just
want everybody to remember Henry Aaron.
—HANK AARON

I earned over one million dollars in my first year out
of college telling the people of America about Lawrence
of Arabia.
—LOWELL THOMAS

I hold that a man had better be dead than alive when
his work is done.
—ALICE CARY

It was easy to understand why Duke Ellington was
called Duke. For even in a pull—over sweater, he was
still an aristocrat.

It gave you a feeling of security—you felt that no matter
how much the world changed and seemed to get away from

you as you grew older, one thing in your life would stay the same.
—MARY DOWELL
(speaking of Harry Truman——sitting in his study, reading, by the little lamp that was always shining in his window)

It's a hard   fact of life that man can adjust to almost anything.
—ALBIE BAKER

I have never met a man who has given me as much trouble as myself.
— DWIGHT L. MOODY

I love you not only for what you are, but for what I am when I'm with you.
—MARY CAROLYN DAVIES

I keep my private life private.
—FIDEL CASTRO

I insist on the right to be smarter today than I was yesterday.
—KONRAD ADENAUER

In the very act of looking into a mirror, we change our whole expression and appearance. So a looking—glass scrunity never shows us how we appear to other people.
—SYDNEY J. HARRIS

I'm a people person. When I travel I like to talk to people and see their homes, rather than visit museums and buildings.
—FERNE CONE

I've never had a golf stick in my hand. I've never

had time. I've always had too many other things to do.
—SAM ERVIN

I guess I am just naturally not energetic. I like to sit around and talk.
—CALVIN COOLIDGE

I would rather be a poor man in a garret with plenty of books than a king who did not love reading.
—THOMAS MACUALAY

I was an under-privileged child, but didn't know it, because I had never seen a privileged child.
—SAM LEVENSON

If you constantly compare yourself with others, you may become either unhappy or boastfully proud. For there will always be people greater or lesser than you.

I don't have stage fright on opening night. I just think: if they could do what I can do, they'd be up here doing it.
—ETHEL MERMEN

I have no regrets about quitting when I did. My heart was breaking when I walked off the stage for the last time. But I wanted to quit while people still wanted to see me. I made up my mind to step into the wings while the audience was still applauding.
—MARY PICKFORD

I've never met a man I didn't like.
—WILL ROGERS

It matters not how a man dies, but how he lives.
—Dr. SAMUEL JOHNSON

I don't know who my grandfather was; I am much more concerned to know what his grandson will be.
—ABRAHAM LINCOLN

I haven't arrived anywhere——I'm only on the way.
—DUKE ELLINGTON   (at the height of his career)

If you haven't got anything nice to say about any—body, come, sit next to me.
—ALICE ROOSEVELT LONGWORTH

If you can trust a man, a written contract is a waste of paper. If you can't trust him, a written contract is still a waste of paper.
—J. PAUL GETTY

I am quite satisfied with my life. I managed to live through the revolution. My personal life was happy. And if there were difficult moments——who has not had difficult moments?
—NADEZHDA KRUPSKAYA
(wife of Lenin)

I was hoisted by my own petard; desserts are now a standard part of my show.
—GRAHAM KERR

I didn't even vote for Jimmy Carter——I'm a Republican!
—MISS LILLIAN
   (Jimmy Carter's mother)

I still find each day too short for all the thoughts I want to think, all the walks I want to take, all the books I want to read, all the friends I want to see.
—JOHN BURROUGHS

I am a slow walker, but I never walk backwards.
—ABRAHAM LINCOLN

It's certain that fine women eat a crazy salad with their meat.
—WILLIAM BUTLER YEATS

I learned long ago to live with pain and fatigue.
—CHARLES STEINMETZ

It takes a person who is wide awake to make his dreams come true.
—ROGER BABSON

I used to think that men were luckier than women in this world. But no more. I'm glad I'm a woman. They have many more options today than men.
—Dr. SONYA FRIEDMAN

It's better to be looked over than overlooked.
—MAE WEST

I don't mind going on a trip if I can be home by noon.
—CHARLES SCHULZ

I saw a man over one hundred years old. His basic diet was sardines and crackers. We all eat too much.
—BERNARD JENSEN

I think people miss an awful lot by being able to see everything. I was so much more tolerant before. Now, if I look at someone who is fat, I wonder why they are. And when I go to church, I don't get nearly as much out of the sermon. There are too many distractions.
—PAULINE COOK MARTIN   (blind for the first 26 years
of her life)

61

I hate the word old. I always use older. Getting old is frightening. Getting older is wonderful.
—JOHN PRINS

I like to do my writing in the early morning hours. That is because there are no negative vibrations floating around. People have not yet started their negative thinking.
—Dr. GEORGE HALL

I'm like a child at Christmas when I go into a library. I'm an intellectual geek. I devour books alive and screaming.
—JOHN KIRTLEY
        (with an IQ of 173)

I'll never forget what's his name.
—JIM HARTZ

I wouldn't have a joint account with even the Angel Gabriel.
—LADY BIRD JOHNSON

I never think of people as black, or white, or yellow, or Jews or Gentiles——people are people, and no two are alike.
—ROD MCKUEN

I've never mastered the alphabet. Why should I? I see no reason why the letters should fall in any certain order.
—PABLO PICASSO

I'm not funny. I just make it possible for other people to be funny.
—BOB BARKER

I didn't pay my dues——I didn't change my name;
I didn't have my teeth capped— I didn't have my nose
straightened.
—BARBRA   STREISAND

I don't have any mysterious powers;   my feats could
be performed by any child of 6 with 60 years of experience
—JOSEPH DUNNINGER, MAGICIAN

I would ask for tomorrow.
—SOLDIER ON BATTLEFIELD
      (when asked what he would wish for)

I am only an average man, but, by George, I work
harder at it than does the average man.
—PRESIDENT THEODORE ROOSEVELT

It's not hard for a leader to do what is right. It's hard
for him to know what is right.
—FRANKLIN ROOSEVELT

It will be a freer life.   Presumably, no one will be
interested in our garbage any more.   That was the only
thing that really outraged me.   It's the end of all privacy
when someone starts going through your garbage.
—NANCY KISSINGER

I could feel the twinkle of his eyes in his handshake.
—HELEN KELLER
      (on meeting Mark Twain)

If you don't have problems, my friends, you're either
dead or you sit in a corner 24 hours a day.
—ROBERT HEYER

I stopped drinking, and for the first time in forty

years, I knew what it was like to wake up in the morning
feeling good.
—DORIS MADSEN

I've simply become color blind. I've become as dark
as most of my friends, and even the little black babies
are no longer afraid of me.
—MISS LILLIAN
(Peace Corps volunteer in India)

I like to see a man proud of the place in which he
lives; I like to see a man live so that his place will be
proud of him.
—ABRAHAM LINCOLN

I'd rather have you sing out of tune and move me,
than sing every note perfectly and sound like you're reading
the stock report. Hate me or love me, but react to me!
—NORMAN LUBOFF

I had success and security——but it wasn't enough.
—INGRID BERGMAN

I am not bound to win but I am bound to be true. I
must stand with anybody that stands right; and part with
him when he goes wrong.
—ABRAHAM LINCOLN

I've had an exciting life. I married for love and got
a little money along with it.
—ROSE KENNEDY

If your house is up for sale, have bread baking in the
oven when the bell rings.
—RUTH RISER

I was fortunate, because I was born with an abundance

64

of energy, drive, vitality, and a zest for life.
—KATHARINE HEPBURN

If you would be interesting, be interested.
—RICHARD ALAN

I was very keen to scale Mt. Everest. I wanted to
see everything. But the ascent almost took my life. I
reached home exhausted. I have decided to climb no more.
—JUNKO TABEI

If this white man wants to live in peace with the Indian
he can. Treat all men alike. Give them an even chance
to live and grow. All men were made by the Great Spirit
Chief. They are all brothers.
—CHIEF JOSEPH

I suppose I must accept that what happens   to me can
be newsworthy regardless of context. Anyway, the time to
get anxious is when nobody's interested at all.
—PRINCE CHARLES OF ENGLAND

I have to have some passion in my life. For me, it's
bridge.
—OMAR SHARIF

It's not the size of the man in the fight; but it's the
size of the fight in the man.

I never did give anybody hell. I just told the truth,
and they thought it was hell.
—HARRY S. TRUMAN

Judgment of the people is often wiser than the wisest
men.
—LOUIS KOSSUTH

Just when I'm wondering whether I'm going to make

it through the day, the American Medical Association comes along to ask if I am interested in learning how to live to be one hundred.
—TOM HORTON

Know thyself.
—SIGMUND FREUD

Keep up with yourself and not someone else. One of our worst hang—ups is to try to keep up with prestige symbols which rob us of self-respect and make us second fiddle to other people.
—Dr. MAXWELL MALTZ

Lonely as his life had been, Hans Christian Anderson did not know that other men, too, have a child deep inside them.

Let everyone you meet, however humble, feel that you regard him as a person of importance.
—WILLARD E. GIVENS

Learn to be happy with people for what they are, and not unhappy with them for what they are not.

Luckiest he is who knows just when to rise and go home.
—JOHN HAY

My father did teach me that, to be a really good farmer, you have to work harder, dig deeper furrows, plant the best seed you can afford, just a little deeper than your neigh— bor. And you work around the clock until the harvest.
—LAWRENCE WELK

Make sure your woman digs your horn.
—LOUIS ARMSTRONG

Man must endure his own suffering, or the suffering of others. Man can't not suffer.
—Dr. KARL BARTH

May you live as long as you want to, and want to as long as you live.
—ROGER MOORE

Men show their character in nothing more clearly than by what they think laughable.
—JOHANN VON GOETHE

Nobody, my darling, could call me a fussy man——But I do like a little bit of butter on my bread!
—ALAN ALEXANDER MILNE

No one outlives his moment of greatness so quickly as an indespensable man.

No labor is sufficient to tire me. I am never weary of being useful.
—LEONARDO DA VINCI

No man is useless while he has a friend.
—ROBERT LOUIS STEVENSON

Nobody is so poor that he has to sit on a pumpkin. That is shiftlessness.
—HENRY DAVID THOREAU

No excellent soul is exempt from a mixture of madness.
—ARISTOTLE

Now, voyager, sail thou forth to seek and find.
—WALT WHITMAN

Never praise a sister to a sister.
—RUDYARD KIPLING

One bad general does better than two good ones.
—NAPOLEON

Only the pure at heart can make a good soup.
—LUDWIG VAN BEETHOVEN

Old age is not for sissies.

One man with courage makes a majority.
—ANDREW JACKSON

Open your eyes and look for some man, or some work for the sake of men, which needs a little time, a little friendliness, a little sympathy, a little human toil. See if there is not some place where you may invest your humanity.
—ALBERT SCHWEITZER

People learn to avoid the things they are hit with.
—ROBERT F. MAGER

People are lonely because they build walls instead of bridges.
—JOSEPH NESTON

People you love never really die.

Russian women marry only for love. We already have economic security. Besides, most of the men we meet have salaries similar to ours. No, we Russian women marry only for love.
—MASHA

Regularity is what's important. Find out what is comfortable to you and stick to it. Don't try to keep adjus—ting. Irregularity is the worst thing for you.

Sometimes our light goes out, but is blown again to flame

by an encounter with another human being.
—ALBERT SCHWEITZER

So far as I know this distinction was earned entirely by my straightening my tie and putting on a jacket just before the TV camera turns on every night. What they don't know, of course, is that my unseen pants still fall in the category of baggy—tweeds.
—WALTER CRONKITE
(on being chosen one of the nation's best dressed men)

Sooner or later, the man who thinks he can, can.
—ARNOLD PALMER

The secret of the demagogue; to make himself seem as stupid as his audience so that they believe they are as clever as he.
—KARL KRAUS

The fellow who worries about what people think of him, wouldn't worry so much if he only knew how seldom they do.

There's no way to pretend being happy if you aren't.
—POLLY BERGEN

The person is always too small for the crime.

To rise at six, to dine at ten,
To sup at six, to sleep at ten,
Makes a man live for ten times ten.
—VICTOR HUGO

The ideal man bears the accidents of life with dignity and grace, making the best of the circumstances.
—ARISTOTLE

Today I get to play golf with some friends. It's a real

event. If I could play anytime, I'd hate it.
–MILTON BERLE

The black man has achieved such outstanding success in sports—not because he was stronger, but because he was hungrier.
–PAUL HARVEY

The man who said that must have been an intellectual. An ordinary man couldn't have been that wrong.
–GEORGE ORWELL

The worst turns the best to the brave.
–ROBERT BROWNING

There is ever the difference between the wise and the unwise; the latter wonders at the unusual; the wise man wonders at the usual.
–RALPH WALDO EMERSON

The most I can do for my friend is simply to be one.
–HENRY DAVID THOREAU

There are two things people cannot stand in this world; success in other people, and success in themselves.

The eyes that shine good morning may be filled with tears at night.

To entertain some people, all you have to do is listen.
–BERNARD EDINGER

Too many people keep looking forward to the good old days.
–ARNOLD H. GLASOW

Those who never quote, in return are seldom quoted.
–ISAAC D'ISRAELI

There are no warlike peoples———
Just warlike leaders.
—RALPH J. BUNCHE

Thy friend has a friend, and thy friend's friend has a friend; be discreet.
—TALMUD

There are three kinds of people; those who make things happen, those who watch things happen, and those who have no idea what happened.

There's no such thing as a good Amos and a bad Andy.
—JOE GARAGIOLA

There are no uninteresting people.
—VALENTINA LEONTYEVA

Unto whom much is given, of him is much expected.
—ROSE KENNEDY

We only think when we are confronted with a problem.
—VERN MILLER

When there's standing room only, it doesn't make much difference whether you're 19 or 90.
—PRINCE PHILIP

We're not prepared to live until we're prepared to die.
—FRANCOIS VOLTAIRE

When you ask me how old I am, I say, "I'm not."
—Dr. RICHARD BALM

When you're all alone, everything belongs to you. But when you have a companion, only half belongs to you.
—LEONARDO DA VINCI

71

Women are wiser than men because they know less and understand more.
—JAMES STEPHENS

When people ask you for critism, really they want praise.
—W. SOMERSET MAUGHAM

What's retirement? Retire to what? I work to keep alive. How much golf can you play in one day?
—GEORGE BURNS

We die from our feet up.   Exercise! Walk! Run! But exercise!
—BERNARD JENSEN

When I was a child, my mother said to me, "If you become a soldier, you'll be a general. If you become a monk, you'll be the Pope." Instead, I became a painter and wound up as Picasso.
—PABLO PICASSO

We have all of us sufficient fortitude to bear the mis—fortunes of others.
—LA ROUCHEFOUCAULD

When I walks, I walks slowly. When I sits, I sits loosely. And when I feel a worry comin' on, I just goes to sleep.
—OLD FRIEND OF PRESIDENT JOHNSON

When A talks about B, one learns more about A than about B.

We do not stop playing because we grow old; we grow old because we stop playing.

You only tease people you like.
—MARGARET BOYD

You've reached middle age when all you exercise is caution.

You are three persons. There is the man you think you are. The man I think you are, and the man you really are.
—FRANCOIS VOLTAIRE
(who once refused to take part in a discussion with a friend because he said there were too many persons around, in fact, six)

You talk funny.
—(Small child from Georgia, visiting President Carter at the White House)

You have gone and there is a terrible desperation in my aloneness——until I remember there is an even more desperation in some people's togetherness.
—LOIS WYSE

As we slosh bravely ahead into the future, we need to be bolstered by words of inspiration from our leaders and our thinkers.
—DENNY MACGOUGAN

As I walked by myself, I talked to myself,
And myself, he said unto me:
Beware of thyself, take care of thyself.
For nobody careth but thee.
—WILLARD E. GIVENS

He that reigns within himself and rules his passions, desires and fears, is more than a king.
—JOHN MILTON

It is magnificant to grow old, if one keeps young while

73

doing it.
—HARRY EMERSON FOSDICK

More often than not we don't want to know ourselves, don't want to depend on ourselves, and don't want to live with ourselves. By middle life most of us are accomplished fugitives from ourselves.
—JOHN W. GARDNER

Man was created——not in jest or at random——but for a great and worthwhile purpose.
—Dr. JAMES FADIMAN

No man can make you feel inferior without your consent.
—ELEANOR ROOSEVELT

People tend to take you the way you take yourself.
—BARBARA MCCLURE WHITE

People do not realize how much they could influence others simply by remembering things they see, hear, or read, Whether in business, social functions or casual conversations, there are ways in which men can dominate each situation by this ability to remember.

Somewhere, someplace, someone is practicing.   And when you meet him, he will win.
—JERRY WEST

Some people disclaim their natural habitat. I always name my origin. It hasn't held me back, and neither has my color. I was born in poverty. Now they've named a park for me in Chester, Pennsylvania.
—ETHEL WATERS

Two men looked out from prison bars———
One saw mud; the other saw stars.

74

The Watergate Conspirators—not one was black; not one had long hair; not one was under thirty; and not one was a woman.
—SARGENT SHRIVER

Time is the coin of your life. It is the only one you have, and only you can determine how it will be spent. Be careful lest you let other people spend it for you.
—CARL SANDBURG

What we do today is what we are tomorrow.
—GLYNN ROSS

We need the touch of wildness in our lives. We are earnest to explore all things. . .to see life pasturing where we never wander.
—HENRY DAVID THOREAU

PLACES

Absolutely nothing happened on this spot.
—WILLIAM O. DOUGLAS
(sign before his home at Goose Prairie, Washington—
population, 8)

America ain't what's wrong with the world.
—GOLDEN

As we say out west, you have earned your spurs.
—JOSEPH MONTOYA

Anyone who drives a car in Manhattan is either very
rich or crazy.
—ERIC SEVAREID

American has always been revolutionary——
when we stop revolting we stop being America.
—HUBERT HUMPREY

Alaska——that great land.　After you've seen it, every—
thing else looks like Kansas.
—HOWARD LINDSAY

A trek to Africa in Livingstone's time would be equiva—
lent to a landing on Venus today.
—TOM JEAL

As my eyes search the prairie, I feel the summer in
the spring.

Ah so!　How you say 'finger-lickin' good in Japan?
—LOY WESTON

All a man from China can really say; I made the tea.
—RALPH WALDO EMERSON

America is the only country in the world where the

people will ride to the poor house in their Cadillacs, wearing
furs coats and diamond rings.
—WILL ROGERS

A man travels the world over in search of what he
needs, and returns home to find it.
—GEORGE MOORE

An umbrella is of no avail against a Scottish mist.
—SYDNEY J. HARRIS

Atlanta is too busy to fight.
—MAYNARD JACKSON

A man should know something of his own country, too,
before he goes abroad.
—LAURENCE STERNE

America has the highest standard of living,
and almost the lowest standard of dying.
—SYDNEY J. HARRIS

A country in which people actually try to become the
mayor of New York City, can't be all bad.
—HOWARD K. SMITH

But I prefer Camp David.
—GERALD R. FORD
(after his visit to Peking)

Bohemia is nothing more than the little country in
which you do not live.
—O. HENRY

Being an English teacher, I have always taught my students not to use "Americanese." But I have discovered

that you have a whole new language here.
—MISS ALICE SMITH, TEACER FROM SCOTLAND

But I don't go there anymore. There is no more dancing, no ice statues dripping champagne, no Henry Thiele in a tall white hat.
—RUTH STRONG
(describing a once beautiful hotel on the Columbia River——
    now a Senior Citizens' Center)

Boston is a state of mind.
—MARK TWAIN

Buckingham Palace? Why, it's about as big as Plains, Georgia.
—CHIP CARTER

But, Billy, aren't you most needed in the asphalt jungles of Manhattan?
—PAUL HARVEY
(Billy Graham planning a crusade to Communist Hungary)

Cannery Row in Monterey, California, is a poem, a stink, a grating noise, a quality of living, a tone, a habit, a nostal-gia, a dream.
—JOHN STEINBECK

Columbus set out trying to find better trade relations with China, and found the New World quite by accident. What we do by accident is often more exciting than what we do on purpose.
—JIM DUNN

Chicago in July isn't too appealing.
—GRACE KELLY

Children born in Cathlamet, Washington, don't leave

after they are grown   They just stay, and they always have.
It is a community of people who have known one another all
their lives.   There couldn't be a better place to live.
—JULIA BUTLER HANSEN

Californians are not merely inhabitants of a state.   They
are a race of people.

Death is not more still than is this Virginia land in the
hour when the sun has sunk away, and it is black beneath
the trees.
—MARY JOHNSTON

Despite the lack of luxuries in China, everyone has
shelter, food, clothing, and a job.   There is far less worry
in China than in other places.
—ANN TOMPKINS

Don't spoil your beautiful Northwest—
and don't let anybody else spoil it.
—DOUG KIKER

Do what you can here where you are—at this moment—you
don't have to move to somewhere else to be part of the solu-
tion.
—PHYLLIS DILLER

Do I think of my climb of Mt. Everest, you ask
Practically never.   It's what I'm doing today—
and what I'm going to do tomorrow.
—SIR EDMUND HILLARY

"Elle est charmante."
—JULIA CHILD
(on her first visit to Seattle)

Each time I visit my boyhood home, it seems to grow

smaller than my memory of it. If I come back often enough, it would look like a doll house.
—MARK TWAIN

Everyone in Washington carries brief cases, and all that is in them is peanut butter sandwiches.
—GEORGE WALLACE

East is East, and West is San Francisco.
—O. HENRY

Every place on earth has its own peculiar beauty; we must enjoy where we are and not be unhappy because we are not somewhere else.
—BRUCE COWAN

Even much—maligned DDT is necessary for some pur—poses. Without it, you can kiss the East Coast good—bye.
—JERRY BAKER

Everyone is so polite in San Francisco. Like they wait in line for everything. I just moved here from Israel and they don't wait in line there.
—NESTER ADAMS

Everything is here, the time, the weather and worthiness are all being summed up and the judgment day is the next few days. Which way it goes doesn't matter now. The adventure is about over. The summit being the little extra everyone wants and so few get.
—RON FEAR
(lost on a climbing expedition in South America)

For every man, high or low, at every St. Helena, there is an element of bitterness, an element of paranoia, an ele—ment of grandiose fantasy life.
—MAX LERNER

French food is the greatest food in the world.
—GAEL GREENE

For twenty years I looked forward to getting out of Washington, D. C.—while my father was the Senator from Missouri, the vice—president, and president. I don't like Washington. I never did. And I hated it in the White House.
—MARGARET TRUMAN

God made the country, and man made the town.
—WILLIAM COWPER

Go west, young man, and grow up with the country.
—JOHN SOULE

Greece is still a real bargain. Come and see us.
—GEORGE THEODORAKOPOULOS

God bring you to a fairer place than even Oxford town.
—WILIFRED MARY LETTS

Heaven is under our feet as well as over our heads.
—HENRY DAVID THOREAU

Historic places give a modern city its flavor. So why do we tear them all down? Every city now looks the same, the same high—rise buildings, the same supermarkets, the same freeways——whether you're in St. Louis, Pittsburgh, or Seattle.
—JULIA CHILD

Home is where the heart is.
—PLINY THE YOUNGER

Henry Thoreau never got very far from Walden Pond, but he learned much about the meaning of life. And he didn't

have to go to New York, or Chicago, or Los Angeles to figure things out.
—NORMAN VINCENT PEALE

Hollywood is a great place if you're an orange.
—FRED ALLEN

In California, at parties all the talk is about money. In New York, it's about the human dilemma.   People of New York are much more in touch with the reality of being alive.
—SHIRLEY MACLAINE

I believe that we are lost here in America, but I believe we shall be found.
—THOMAS WOLFE

If you're going to have a heart attack, be sure to have it in Seattle.

In Sweden this would have been impossible. There is no opportunity for a commoner to attend a banquet for a king.
—KING CARL GUSTAF,   dining with 600 persons in Seattle

It is my belief, Watson, that the vilest alleys of London do not present a more dreadful record of sin than does the smiling and beautiful country—side.
—SIR ARTHUR CONAN DOYLE

I believe in private property. Russians share everything, income, food, clothing, living. They live a communal life at the foundation. That's why I left Russia.
—SVETLANA PETERS
(daughter of Stalin)

I remember our first drive through Central Park——in a

lazy clip—clop carriage.   Now we speed through the park as we speed through our days——and I wonder whatever became of the driver, the horse, and us.
—LOIS WYSE

It's the best country in the world. I feel like I'd like to have a cup of tea, and a good cry.
—HELEN REDDY
   (on becoming a citizen of the United States)

I can be comfortable almost anywhere, but I like the 24—hour room service in Europe and China. But I love love love coming home best of all.
—BARBARA WALTERS

In Alaska, in the early days,   the natives passed the visitors on from one to another, and you were never there without a friend.
—JANE BARNES

If you live in a small town, not too far from a big city, you are having the best of two worlds.
—ROBERT W. BUNKE

I was born in the most remote corner of the earth.
—NICOLAUS COPERNICUS
   (born in Thorn, Prussian Poland)

It's like being in Fatchburg, Massachusetts, during the last week of the campaign.
—JOAN KENNEDY
   (visiting Leningrad)

In Washington D.C., three months is a generation.
—NEIL MACNEIL

I turned my back on Fuji, and left my homeland. But when I set eyes on Mt. Rainier, I knew I was all right.
—FUMI KIMURA

If you want a basic reason why people keep coming and returning, I guess I would have to say it is the people of Hana.
—JOSEPHINE MEDEIROS

It is raining rain to the West.
It is raining torrents in the East.
It is sprinkling drops out of the stars——in Hawaii.

I find my greatest solace walking in the Grand Canyon, because there I think I am closer to God and His peacefulness than any other place I know.
—BARRY GOLDWATER

I think everyone who visits San Francisco, leaves a part of him there when he leaves.
—BETTY WHITE

In the Pacific Northwest, our weather is our way of life.
—KEN KEENER

I will never leave California for too long, even if I have to go back earning $75 a week. Boy, those were the days!
—JOSEPH COTTON

If you have a song in your heart, the state of Connecticut is interested in you.

I can think of no place except Honolulu, where you can stand on the street corner and see people from every nation in the world going by.
—NORMAN GEORGE

I want to return to my Texas ranch and sit in the cedar—brakes for awhile——and just think.
—LEON JAWARSKI

I never saw a town where everything is so close together, and yet everyone does so much driving.
—RON YATES
(speaking of Pullman, Washington)

In New York I feel too crowded to swing a dead cat.
—LYNDON B. JOHNSON

I would never have hit the big time if it hadn't been for all my experiences on the farm of North Dakota.
—LAWRENCE WELK

I boil with anger at the ravages of tree burning to open up land in Brazil, while people go around making fancy speeches on Tree Day.
—DOM PEDRO.

In California a treatment center for sea birds rescued from a coastal oil slick, played a recording of the surf twen—ty—four hours a day, to make the sea birds feel at home.

It takes real skill to go from driving a car in California to driving a car in Detroit.
—ARTHUR HAILEY

It is easy to locate the United States, but finding America is a little more difficult.

It's a knock at yourself if you knock your town; it isn't your town—it's you.

In the United States, a fish is a fish;

In the Puget Sound a fish is a salmon.
—GOVERNOR DIXIE LEE RAY

Is it not marvelous how far afield some of us are willing to travel in pursuit of that beauty which we leave at home?
—DAVID GRAYSON

In British Columbia a handshake is stronger than a writ-ten contract.
—ADA ADSHEAD

I made it to 100 because I lived my critical years in sun-ny California.

Indiana isn't as far away as people think.
—WALLY BRUNER

I still find New York very exciting. I wouldn't live any-where else.
—ARLENE FRANCIS

It's almost impossible to get a bad dinner in San Francisco.
—HARRY REASONER

I wish sports were like they used to be in England. We'd get together for a bowling on the green, a little feed, and a smoke and a talk session.   Nobody's got time to do that over here.
—ARTHUR GREEN

It doesn't matter that 34 other American cities are windier than Chicago. People look for wind when they come here and they find what they look for.
—SYDNEY J. HARRIS

I love America as she is——not as she could be.
—JOHN MCCOOK ROOTS

If you don't like St. Louis weather, just wait a minute.
—MARK TWAIN

I finally made it to New York. This is my kind of life.
I love everything about this dirty, old city; the pavements,
the excitement, the pace, the people.
—MARGARET TRUMAN

Israel——It's aggravating, irritating ——but very exciting!
—FERNE CONE

I would rather live out my life in Clown Alley than in a
marble palace.
—EMMETT KELLY

I think the best parts of my life have been the years
I've spent with the Indians of my state, as I've been privi-
leged to watch them retain their beautiful culture.
—BARRY GOLDWATER

In Boston they ask, "How much does he know?"
In New York, "How much is he worth?"
In Philadelphia, "Who were his parents?"
—MARK TWAIN

In traveling, a man must carry knowledge with him if he
would bring home knowledge.
—SAMUEL JOHNSON

I never left home.
—BOB HOPE
(on his first trip to Russia)

If I could live any place in the whole world, I would live on the Columbia River, not far from The Bridge of the Gods.
—RUTH STRONG

It is always sunrise somewhere.
—JOHN MUIR

I was born in the most favored spot on earth, the village of Concord, Massachusetts. And just in the nick of time too.
—HENRY DAVID THOREAU

I love California. I love the sun and the sea. And most of all I love the lifestyle. Everyone has his own style here. No one cares whether anyone is watching. Each does his own. Watch or not——who cares?
—SVETLANA ALLILUYEVA
(Joseph Stalin's daughter)

I have no relish for the country; it is a kind of healthy grave.
—SYDNEY SMITH

I've got to get out of Los Angeles before I'm clawed to death by smog and traffic. I want to sit on a porch in the country and see the stars.
—VICKI LAWRENCE

In order to get along in the desert you must accept the desert the way it is.
—FLETCHER

I can still hear the stillness.
—EMILY KIMBROUGH
(on a boat trip through Ireland)

90

I love this country, where people know when you are sick, love you while you are alive, and miss you when you die.
—LYNDON BAINES JOHNSON
(speaking of his Texas Hill country)

I'll go on speaking just the way I spoke in Arkansas. And it doesn't matter if people in Brooklyn can't understand me, because I can't understand them, either.
—DIZZY DEAN

Japan will inherit the earth——because they have learned to live with nature—not try to control it.
—DR. SVINTH

K2 has only been seen a few times and that intrigues me. And K2 is far enough away from Everest (some 700 miles) to have its own charisma.
—LOU WHITTAKER

London is where it's at.
—PERLE MESTA

Ma sunburned the roof of her mouth looking at the New York skyscrapers.
—CARL TROTTER

Marco Polo discovered spaghetti in China.
—BEN LIN

Most people have a favorite city. I have two. London and San Francisco.
—ALLISTAIR COOKE

My favorite thing to do in New England is to take a walk through the birches. In Monaco I sometimes feel hemmed in. I can't walk out the door and take a stroll through the birches.
—GRACE KELLY

Marriage is a damnable serious business, especially around Boston.
—JOHN PHILLIPS MARZUAND

Mother Russia, let us do things for ourselves.
—PEOPLE OF ROMANIA

New York is one of those cities whose treasures yield most generously to those who seek on foot.
—ROBIN MCCABE

Out in Michigan we don't have crabs, but we do have a few crabby people.
—GERALD FORD

Of course we're excited about the coming of the First Family for a skiing holiday at Vail, Colorado. But we're more excited about the coming of the snow.
—SKI INSTRUCTOR

On the whole, I'd rather be in Philadelphia.
—W. C. FIELDS

The earth is our all. Let's not fumble the ball.
—ELSA V. MAREST

There are no sunsets anywhere in the world like a sunset in Fallon, Nevada.
—ELLA WILSON

There are great and small people all over the world. But it looks to me like they are mostly big people in Waseca, Minnesota.
—DAVID KUNST
(walking around the world)

The mystery of man's past will be unraveled in Africa.
—CHARLES DARWIN

92

The healthiest spot in America is a stretch of corn and cattle country in south—central Nebraska, and what people do there to live longer than the rest of us, nobody knows.
—JOAN YOUNGER DICKINSON

The time to enjoy a European trip is about three weeks after unpacking.

There were only I, the river, and the towering canyon walls. Nature and I were one.
—BRUCE COWAN

The best thing was the tea.
—TOURIST IN THE ORIENT

The decline of manners in America bothers me——the rudeness——a young person sitting like a lump when an older person enters the room. And when I go to Europe, who's making all the noise? Americans. And in Paris——who pinched my bottom? An American, of course!
—GLORIA SWANSON

The White House was his prison, but the Texas ranch was his home.
—FRANK REYNOLDS
(speaking of President Johnson)

There's more to Denmark than a piece of Danish.
—MOGEN EDSBERG

The coldest winter I ever spent was the summer I spent in California.
—JAMES WHITCOMB RILEY

Once a year we have to get back to Idaho to go back packing in the woods, and sort of recharge our batteries.
—SENATOR FRANK CHURCH

People have said I could set up housekeeping on the Sahara Desert and anyone walking in after I'd been there fifteen minutes could tell I came from New England.
—BETTE DAVIS

Perhaps the forests of Amazonia will remain when the human dynasty has passed.

People in England always rise to a crisis. Some say they even create a crisis to rise to.

Russia is a riddle—wrapped in a mystery, inside an enigma.
—WINSTON CHURCHILL

Singapore has become Asia's cleanest city, but it's so dull. W. C. Fields could easily have preferred being in Philadelphia.
—PETER O'LOUGHLIN

South America presents the most fantastic and seemingly insoluble picture in the world. Left and right are all mixed up. That's where I'm going to do a novel.
—REID BUCKLEY

Summer in Monaco seems to go on forever, and I'm not particularly a summer person.
—GRACE KELLY

San Francisco is the only city where you can wear black anywhere, any time, and any place.
—MARIAN YOUNG

Tokyo is big and gray and sprawling, and not attractive. But then there is Kyoto-ah, there is refreshment for the soul.
—BARBARA WALTERS

Two years away from America is like being away forever.

You come back, and everything is different.   You feel different rhythms.
—LAUREN BACALL

When I was travelling in Egypt, most of the tourists were Americans, and most of the Americans were school teachers.
—DAVID BRINKLEY

When a man is tired of London, he is tired of life; for there is in London all that life can afford.
—SAMUEL JOHNSON

When I was a young boy in Hoboken, New Jersey, I thought it was a great boot if I could get a glimpse of the mayor in a parade.   Now, entertaining at the White House for the President has been quite a boot for me.
—FRANK SINATRA

When you're in Texas, always shuck the tamale.
—GERALD R. FORD

When I was a kid, I used to dream about travelling as far away as Gary, Indiana.   Now I'm using Bangkok for a laundry drop.   You haven't lived until you've had an elephant give you room service.
—BOB HOPE

Watergate?   I've never heard of it.   I'm from Wales.
—LYDIA PORTER

When I am in the country I wish to vegetate like the country.
—WILLIAM HAZLITT

What I like most about Monaco is living by the sea. What I dislike most is that autumn never comes.
—GRACE KELLY

If it hadn't been for all my experience down on the farm

in North Dakota, I never could have been President of the United States.
—TEDDY. ROOSEVELT

It couldn't have happened anywhere but in little old New York.
—O. HENRY

It makes Niagara Falls look like a kitchen faucet.
—ELEANOR ROOSEVELT
(viewing Iguassu Falls in South America)

New York City is enchanting, divine, and awfully, terribly friendly. I love your very nice bobbies.
—AUDREY BROMMEL

There is nothing wrong with America that Americans can't set it right.
—NELSON ROCKEFELLER

We are just a tiny planet in space and we're all just hanging on because of a six mile chunk of bioshpere that cloaks us. It is a very tenuous arrangement, indeed, and it makes one realize we must all be brothers and act like brothers.
—BILL MOYERS

All places are distant from heaven alike.
—ROBERT BURTON

THINGS

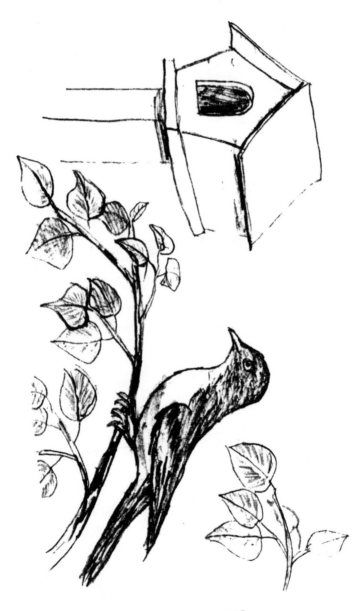

The falling of a teacup puts us out of temper for the day; and a quarrel that commenced about the pattern of a gown may end only with our lives.
—WILLIAM HAZLITT

We learn from history that we learn nothing from history.
—GEORGE BERNARD SHAW

All my possessions for a moment of time.
—QUEEN ELIZABETH I

An airplane is the safest form of transportation with the possible exception of the elevator.
—FRANK BORMAN

A happy marriage is not so much finding the right person as being the right person.
—MARABEL MORGAN

And airplane food? When I fly I bring my own sandwiches.
—JULIA CHILD

As one who cons at evening o'er an album, all alone , And muses on the faces of the friends that he has known.
—JAMES WHITCOMB RILEY

Adversity is but an obstacle to be overcome.
—THOMAS A. EDISON

Anything can have a kick to it.
—MARVEL JOHNSON

Always have the house in order by noon.
—MARY WORTH

An excellent way to cope with frustrations of today— open a can of pork and beans; count each bean before chewing it.   Troubles vanish and relief is immediate.
—JEROME TECHTMAN

99

Always wear something you can walk in.
–KATHRYN CROSBY

As scarce as truth is, the supply has always been in excess of the demand.
–JOSH BILLINGS

Any man can write sense—only a gifted few can write nonsense.
–SAMUEL JOHNSON

As a cure for worrying, work is better than whiskey.
–THOMAS EDISON

A man's true wealth is the good he does in this world.
–MOHAMMED

All I need to make me happy is a kitchen, a fireplace, and a garden of flowers.
–BETTE DAVIS

A lifetime of happiness! No man alive could bear it; it would be hell on earth.
–GEORGE BERNARD SHAW

And come he slow, or come he fast,
It is but Death who comes at last.
–SIR WALTER SCOTT

A chuckle has therapeutic value. Try to chuckle very quietly and feel the inward satisfaction.
–IVAH MERWIN DYNES

A suntan may be a status symbol, but it's dangerous. If you don't have chlorophyll in your veins, direct sunlight can do nothing but harm.
–DR. S. W. BECKER

A speech that is read is like a dried flower; the substance indeed is there, but the color is faded and the

perfume is gone.
—LORAIN

A thing to be useful has got to be used. But hated things, sir, are less used than abused.
—ROBERT F. MAGER

Autobiographies ought to begin with Chapter II.
—ELLERY SEDGWICK

Ask yourself whether you are happy. and you cease to be.
—JOHN STUART MILL

A smile is your best face value.
—PAUL HARVEY

All animals are equal, but some animals are more equal than others.
—GEORGE ORWELL

A pat on the back, though only a few vertebrae removed from a kick in the pants, is miles ahead in results.
—BENNETT CERF

After the first death, there is no other.
—DYLAN THOMAS

A rich man's joke is always funny.
T. E. BROWN

All history is but the lengthened shadow of great men.
—RALPH WALDO EMERSON

As long as you have a window, life is exciting.
GLADYS TABER

All about us are emptier cups;
Try filling them and watch your own fill up.
—FRANCES R. HAVERGAL

A problem is not a problem unless you make it a problem.
—EARTHA KITT

Beautiful soup! Who cares for fish, game, or any other dish? Who would not give all else for two pennyworth only of beautiful soup?
—LEWIS CARROLL

But of what use is goodness, if there is no edge to it?
—RALPH WALDO EMERSON

Being cold is a state of mind.
—BART McMATH

Beware of all enterprises that require new clothes.
—HENRY DAVID THOREAU

Be not afraid of greatness; some are born great, some achieve greatness, and some have greatness thrust upon them.
—WILLIAM SHAKESPEARE

Breathing is one of the secrets of youth. People breathe too shallow. The toxics aren't able to leave the body.
—LIZALOTTA BALESCA

Brains are the cheapest commodity you can buy.
—KARL BAUR

Books are not written; they are re-written.
—ALLEN SAUNDERS

Candor can be the subtlest form of deception.
—ERIC SEVAREID

Carrots are truly an amazing vegetable. Do anything to them you want — except to dice them and mix them up with green peas.
—JAMES A. BEARD

Champagne is my least favorite of all drinks. People have been forcing drink on me for years, and I don't like it. It gets to the stage of being quite irritating.
—PRINCESS ANNE OF BRITAIN

Creeping is probably the second best exercise in the world — next to swimming. It's perfect. Creep two or three times a day, two or three minutes each time.
—H. L. HUNT

Colds are strictly in the head. They are psychogenic. There are no germs in drafts — you catch cold from them because you think you will.
—SWIRLINGTON THRUSH

Change means the unknown — it means, too, (many people cry), insecurity. Nonsense! No one from the beginning of time has had security.
—ELEANOR ROOSEVELT

Dignities result from indignities.
—ERIC SEVAREID

Don't dare drink water without chemicals, and don't dare drink water with chemicals.
—PAUL HARVEY

Don't count sheep. Talk to the shepherd.
—HILARY RUBENSTEIN

Democracy is the worst possible form of government, except, of course, all the others.
—WINSTON CHURCHILL

Do not shorten the morning by getting up late. Look upon it as the quintessence of life, as to a certain extent, sacred.
—SCHOPENHAUR

Don't let spices just sit. Use them!
—JAMES A. BEARD

Doors are interesting. They open and close.
—MARJORIE W. SMITH

Enthusiasm may mark the difference between success and failure.
—NORMAN VINCENT PEALE

For it is in the little things that life purposes are directed, and often it is around the corners of contingencies that careers are re-channeled.
—HELEN THEMES RALEY

Famous remarks are seldom quoted correctly.
—SIMEON STRUNSKY

From what is here must become what is to be, for there is no other material.
—GWEN FROSTIC

For a little house — a house of my own,
Out of the wind's and the rain's way.
—PADRAIC COLUM

Few things are harder to put up with than the annoyance of a good example.
—MARK TWAIN

Give me the ready hand rather than the ready tongue.
—GIUSEPPE GARABALDI

Gifts on Christmas, birthdays, anniversary, of course. But the present that shakes away the sagging spirit is one that is offered for no reason at all — on any old ragamuffin of a day.
—GEORGE KENT

Give me again my hollow tree,
A crust of bread, and liberty.
—ALEXANDER POPE

Good music is around — just as it had always been. Lots of it is mediocre; much of it is fine. It's knowing the difference that separates the gold records from the tin whistles.
—BING CROSBY

Give me a for instance.
—R. R. LEGAULT

Go easy with the salt shaker. Remember, salt is used in embalming, so most of us are going around half dead.
GAVIN MACLEOD

Happiness is doing things — rather than possessing things.
—DR. B. F. SKINNER

Home is not where you live, but where they understand you.
—CHRISTIAN MORGENSTERN

Half of the evil in the world is gossip started by good people.
—ED HOWE

He wrapped himself in quotations — as a beggar would enfold himself in the purple of emperors.
—RUDYARD KIPLING

How sickness enlarges the dimensions of a man's self to himself.
—CHARLES LAMB

Health is being unaware of any part of your body.
—HELEN HOWELL

When all else fails, read the directions.

Here's to today. Not yesterday, not tomorrow, but today. These are the good old days — if only we knew what to do with them.
—DOUGLAS FAIRBANKS, JR.

How little security have we when we trust our happiness in the hands of others.
—WILLIAM HAZLITT

Happiness is a way station between too little and too much.
—CHANNING POLLOCK

Home is a place that when you come there, they have to let you in.
—ROBERT FROST

How monotonous the sounds of the forest would be if the music came only from the Top Ten birds.
—DAN BENNETT

Idealism is the noble toga that political gentlemen drape over their will to power.
—ALDOUS HUXLEY

In all tragedy there is a kind of triumph.
—HENRY F. GRAFF

It is not enough to win the fight. We must win that for which we fight.
—ELEANOR ROOSEVELT

It is better to smell easily than to smell sweetly.
—DR. S. ROSS FOX
(Discussing the danger of inhaling too much perfume)

Instead of sitting on opposite sides of the table confronting each other, sit on the same side and confront the problem.
—HOWARD K. SMITH

If you have to ask what jazz is, you'll never know.
—LOUIS ARMSTRONG

It is not hard to find the truth. What is hard is not to run away from it once you have found it.
—GILSON

If a man owns land, the land owns him.
—RALPH WALDO EMERSON

It is the mark of superior minds to disagree and yet be friendly.
—WILLARD E. GIVENS

If you don't like the heat, stay out of the kitchen.
—HARRY S. TRUMAN

If you're emotionally mature, it doesn't matter where you sit in a restaurant.
—GAEL GREENE

I like books. Some of them I also love.
—MALCOLM B. BOYD

If I had to choose, I would rather have birds than airplanes.
—CHARLES A. LINDBERGH

I'm a life-long addict of the comics. I learned to read by sitting beside Grandmother as she read the comics to me. Sunday was the best day of all because the comics were in colour, and there were more.
—PHILIP H. LOVE

If your feet are cold, put on your hat. Really!
—TACOMA MOUNTAINEERS

I always consider applause at the beginning of a speech manifestation of a faith. If it comes in the middle, it's a sign of hope. If it comes at the end, it's always charity.
—BISHOP FULTON J. SHEEN

If you feel the urge to do something for someone—a surprise note, a telephone call,—but you don't do it because you feel you might be intruding—do it anyway.
—ALICE OBERHAUSER

I've never found a weed I couldn't like.
—JERRY BAKER

In cooking, do not overdo your seasoning. Things should taste of what they are. Chicken should taste like chicken. String beans like string beans. You shouldn't be able to say "Oh, nutmeg!"
—LYNN MINTON

I would like to return to the good old days when Mother could recognize baby's runny nose as a runny nose.
—JACK G. SHILLER

It is completely unimportant. That is why it is so interesting.
—AGATHA CHRISTIE

I have no sceptor, but I have a pen.
—VOLTAIRE

I'm against a homogenized society because I want the cream to rise.
—ROBERT FROST

I always wanted to do the big things, but the little things kept getting in the way.
—BESS STREETER ALDRICH

In dinner talk it is perhaps allowable to fling on any fagot rather than let the fire go out.
—J. M. BARRIE

I have other fish to fry.
—CERVANTES

In the kingdom of birds, the parrot is the best talker—and the worst flier.
—ORVILLE WRIGHT

If you admit to middle age, join me in starwishing:
>   Star light, star bright,
>   The first star I see tonight,
>   I wish I may, I wish I might,
>   Have the wish I wish tonight.
—GRACE R. VANDER SLUYS

It is possible to possess too much. A man with one watch knows what time it is. A man with two watches is never sure.
—LEE SEGALL

I'm for it.
—QUEEN ELIZABETH
>   (when asked what she thought of marriage)

If you can't pronounce it, don't eat it.
—DAVID BRINKLEY

If you feel adventurous, try a little celery seed on top.
—ERNEST HEMINGWAY

If you ever need a helping hand, you'll find one at the end of your arm.
—SAM LEVENSON

If you love the world, it will love you back.
—RUBENSTEIN

I'd leave all the hurry, the noise and the fray,
For a house full of books and a garden of flowers.
—ANDREW LANG

I always smell a book. Book smells differ but all are interesting.
—MALCOLM BOYD

I love everything that's old; old friends, old times, old manners, old books, old wines.
—OLIVER GOLDSMITH

I had brains enough to know that certain kinds of shoes were comfortable and that keeping up stockings is uncomfortable.
—KATHARINE HEPBURN
(wearing slacks and sandals long before they were popular)

In character, in manner, in style, in all things, the supreme excellence is simplicity.
—HENRY WADSWORTH LONGFELLOW

It is chiefly through books that we enjoy intercourse with superior minds...In the best books great men talk to us, give us their most precious thoughts, and pour their souls into ours.
—WILLIAM CHANNING

I'm glad you like adverbs—I adore them. They are the only qualifications I really much respect.
—HENRY JAMES

I hate quotations. Tell me what you know.
—RALPH WALDO EMERSON

I like to answer questions up or down.
—ROBERT STRAUSS

It's no use to blame the looking glass if your face is awry.
—NIKOLAI GOGOL

I never forget a suit.
—EARL OTIS

I don't care where you put me in a restaurant, as long as you put my back to the wall.
—GRAHAM KERR

110

If all the year were playing holidays,
To sport would be as tedious as work.
—WILLIAM SHAKESPEARE

It was involuntary. They sunk my boat.
—JACK KENNEDY
(when asked how he became a war hero)

It's a lot better to be stolen from than to have to steal.
—CHARLES SCHULZ

Life is other things than work; it is fun: swimming, buying
antiques, the task of being really married. God! The energy
and concentration that takes, just to relate continuously to
another person.
—ANNE BANCROFT

Love thou the rose, yet leave it on its stem.
—OWEN MEREDITH

Life is short. The sooner that a man begins to enjoy his
wealth the better.
—SAMUEL JOHNSON

Learn to make bread. The rhythm of the kneading is very
soothing. Take primitive comfort in the warm responsiveness
of the dough.
—JOAN MILLS

Love does not consist in gazing at each other, but in looking
outward together in the same direction.
—ANTOINE DE SAINT-EXPERY

Life's too short for chess.
—LORD BYRON

Let down your buckets where you are.
—BOOKER T. WASHINGTON

Let the clean wind blow the cobwebs from your body. Air is medicine.
–LILLIAN RUSSELL

My only fear about old age was that people's minds start to go...But I've been watching mine very closely, and the brain is the toughest organ we have.
–KATHERINE ANNE PORTER

Make wisdom your provision for the journey from youth to old age. It is a more certain support than all other possessions.
–DIOGENES LAERTIUS

Meet success like a gentleman and disaster like a man.
–LORD BIRKENHEAD

May friendship, like wine, improve as time advances; and may we always have old wine, old friends, and young cares.
–HENRY MANCINI

Morals are what you do and manners are how you do it.
–ELIZABETH POST

May you always have jam on your muffin.
–AGNES DICKEY

Make preparations in advance. You don't have trouble if you are prepared for it.
–THEODORE ROOSEVELT

Maturity is the ability to live in someone else's world.
–JAMES WEAVER

My kingdom for an attic. Today's homes have storage space under beds and out in the garage. But attics are for those who save—for those who dream.
–DON DUNCAN

No matter how much cats fight, there always seems to be plenty of kittens.
—ABRAHAM LINCOLN

Nobody, I think, ought to read poetry, or look at pictures, who cannot find a great deal more in them than the poet or or artist has actually expressed.
—NATHANIEL HAWTHORNE

Never give yourself a title. You are Jane Smith, not Miss Jane Smith.
—LEILA LAVIN

Newspapers always excite curiosity. No one ever lays one down without a feeling of disappointment.
—CHARLES LAMB

Never buy what you do not want because it is cheap.
—THOMAS JEFFERSON

Nostalgia isn't what it used to be.
—PETER DEVRIES

Oxen and women didn't have it so good in the good old days.
—DR. OTTO BETTMANN

Obscenity can be found in every book except the telephone directory.
—GEORGE BERNARD SHAW

Oh! It is great to shake off the trammels of the world—and to be known by no other title than the gentleman in the parlor!
—WILLIAM HAZLITT

One great use of words is to hide our thoughts.
—FRANCOIS VOLTAIRE

Oh, you want to know about the governor's mansion? Well,

to tell the truth, it's more like a Safeway Store.
—GOVERNOR JERRY BROWN

Originality is the art of concealing your source.
—FRANKLIN P. JONES

One of the pleasantest things in the world is going on a journey; but I like to go by myself.
—WILLIAM HAZLITT

One of the greatest sounds of them all, and to me it is a sound, is utter, complete silence.
—ANDRE KOSTELANETZ

People can take injustice; what stings is justice.
—EDDIE P. MORGAN

People say that life is the thing, but I prefer reading.
—L. P. SMITH

Plunge boldly into the thing of life! Seize it where you will!
—JOHANN VON GOETHE

Quotations, like books, are true levelers. They give to all, who will faithfully use them, the society, the spiritual presence, of the best and greatest of our race.
—EMILY M. BECK

Remember that the most beautiful things in the world are the most useless; peacocks and lilies, for instance.
—HERMAN MELVILLE

Reading is the most lasting of all life's pleasures.
—SAMUEL COLERIDGE

Sleeping little matters little. What does matter is the anxiety the lack of sleep may produce.
—ALTON BLAKESLEE

Some books are to be tasted, others to be swallowed, and some few to be chewed and digested slowly...
—FRANCIS BACON

Small hinges, indeed! History swings on them.
—HELEN RALEY

Suffering from everyday pressures? Go seek the elements, and they will bear you up again.
—JAMES JOYCE

Show me a hero and I will write you a tragedy.
—F. SCOTT FITZGERALD

Steinmetz's only tools were a tin box of pencils, reams of paper, a canister of cigars, and his mind.
—FLOYD MILLER

Silence is the most perfect expression of scorn.
—GEORGE BERNARD SHAW

Some see things as they are, and say, Why?
I dream of things that could be, and say, Why not?
—ROBERT KENNEDY

Sometimes the best medicine is a tincture of time.
—DR. S. ROSS FOX

The world will never lack for want of wonders—only for want of wonder.
—GILBERT CHESTERTON

There's rosemary, that's for remembrance. . .
And there is pansies, That's for thoughts.
—WILLIAM SHAKESPEARE

There is no house in the world big enough for two women.
—ALICE PALM

115

There is nothing sillier than a silly laugh.
—CATULS

The most beautiful thing we can experience is the mysterious. It is the source of all true art and science.
—ALBERT EINSTEIN

Thank God for tea! How did the world exist without tea? I'm glad I was not born before tea.
—SYDNEY SMITH

Taking note is better than taking notes.
—CLIFF LAYCOCK

There is no such thing as a gift.
—JOHN TYLER

The young man knows the rules, but the old man knows the exceptions.
—OLIVER WENDELL HOLMES

Talent is that which is in a man's power; genius is that in whose power a man is.
—JAMES J. ROUSSEAU

The best armor is to keep out of gunshot.
—SIR FRANCIS BACON

The silences of solitude will mend my weary world.
—MARY CLAUS

The web of our life is of a mingled yarn, good and ill together.
—WILLIAM SHAKESPEARE

There are three things no man can do to the entire satisfaction

another, make love; poke the fire; and run a newspaper.
—WILLIAM ALLEN WHITE

Things worth being are better than things worth having.
—DR. MEYER FRIEDMAN

Thank heavens, the sun has gone in, and I don't have to
go out and enjoy it.
—LOGAN PEARSALL SMITH

The happy heart makes the happy day.
—JUDY COWAN

The only thing that is sure is that nothing is sure.
—ALPHONSE KARR

To be hungry is a devine feeling.
—ANNE-MARIE BENNSTROM

To lose weight, eat:
Breakfast like a king;
Lunch like a prince;
And dinner like a pauper.
—DR. THOREK

To celebrate the 4th of July, our Independence Day, we
will go off to the beach in our Volkswagen-spread out our
Hong Kong blanket, listen to our Taiwan transistor,   and
eat pizza.
—PAUL HARVEY

There is a certain twinge of pleasure in a toothache.
—MARGARET BOYD

The average Ph. D. thesis is nothing but a transference
of bones from one graveyard to another.
—J. FRANK DOBIE

To give the people danceable music was our goal—they didn't have to go to Julliard to understand what we were doing.
—GUY LOMBARDO

The buck stops here.
—HARRY TRUMAN

The difficulty of life is the choice.
—GEORGE MOORE

That all-softening, o'er powering knell,
The tocsin of the soul—the dinner bell.
—LORD BYRON

Using chopsticks without looking at them is real confidence.
—RICHARD NIXON

Words are the most powerful drug used by mankind.
—RUDYARD KIPLING

We have killed more people celebrating Independence Day than we lost fighting for it.
—WILL ROGERS

Wondrous the English language—the language of live men!
DR. SAMUEL JOHNSON

When you put a hat on, it changes your whole role—you feel differently about yourself.
—JIM HARTZ

When all candles be out, all cats be gray.
—JOHN HEYWOOD

When you steal from one author, it's plagiarism; when you steal from many, it's research.
—WILSON MIZNER

When I look at the dawn, I realize the complexities of nature.

The construction of an airplane is a simple thing when compared to the migratory life of a bird.
—CHARLES A. LINDBERG

Water—the best drink there is—and the hardest to get.
—VERN MILLER

What a blessing it is that even in this age of efficiency, there are still some small inexacting household chores that have to be done by hand.
—RACHEL PEDEN

When I don't know the facts, I pound on the law.
When I don't know the law, I pound on the facts.
When I don't know either one, I pound on the table.
—CLARENCE DARROW

When I stopped using my dishwasher, and began washing my dishes in hot soapy water, the arthritis in my hands went completely away.
—PENNY AIKEN

We know more about the stars than we know about rheumatism.
—HENRY HASKINS

When people made pornographic pictures, I made money.
—WALT DISNEY

PROVERBS

120

121

As I walk the trail of life in the fear of the wind and rain,
Grant, O Great Spirit, that I may always walk like a man.
—CHEROKEE INDIAN PRAYER

A man's true wealth is the good he does in this world.
—MOHAMMED

A wise man does not trust all his eggs to one basket.
—CERVANTES

A wise man will make more opportunities than he finds.
—FRANCIS BACON

A man is a lion in his own cause.
—SCOTTISH

A full belly makes a dull brain.
—BENJAMIN FRANKLIN

A good laugh is sunshine in a house.
—WILLIAM THACKERAY

An ill wind blows in favour of the ship that has no destination.
—DR. HANS SELYE

A friend is, one might say, a second self.
—CICERO

A happy life is tranquility of mind.
—CICERO

A handful of common sense is worth a bushel of learning.
—SPANISH

A mile walked with a friend has only one hundred steps.
—RUSSIAN

A good husband makes a good wife.
—ROBERT BURTON

A man shows his character by what he laughs at.
—GERMAN

A barking dog is often more useful than a sleeping lion.
—ARABIAN

As long as the sun shines one does not ask for the moon.
—RUSSIAN

A devoted friendship is never without anxiety.
—MARQUISE DE SEVIGNE

An intelligent enemy is better than a stupid friend.
—AFRICAN

Believe nothing and be on your guard against everything.
—LATIN

Burn not thy fingers to snuff another's candle.
—SCOTTISH

Better ask twice than your way once.
—DANISH

Blessed are those who can give without remembering, and
can take without forgetting.
—ELIZABETH BIBESCO

Bend with the wind and thus survive, though storms may
flatten you. Weep not at fate, but spring erect, as bamboo
thickets do.
—CHINESE BLESSING

Beware the fury of a patient man.
—JOHN DRYDEN

Beware of little expenses. A small leak will sink a great
ship.
—BENJAMIN FRANKLIN

Behind bad luck comes good luck.
—GYPSIES

Content thyself awhile.
Pleasure and action make the hours seem short.
—WILLIAM SHAKESPEARE

Choose your wife, not at a dance, but in the harvest field.
—CZECHOSLOVAK

Cooks never die of starvation.
—RUSSIAN

Don't shoot at the king unless you can kill him.
—RALPH WALDO EMERSON

Debt and misery live on the same road.
—RUSSIAN

Do not unto others that which is hateful to you.
—JEWISH

During his lifetime, an individual should devote his efforts
to create happiness and to enjoy it. Also keep it in store in
society so that individuals of the future may also enjoy it.
—CH' EN TU HSIU

Employ thy time well if thou meanest to gain leisure.
—BENJAMIN FRANKLIN

Examine the neighbourhood before choosing a home.
—ORIENT

Enough is enough, and too much spoils.
—ITALIAN

Everybody thinks of changing humanity, but nobody thinks
of changing himself.
        TOLSTOI

Eat not to dullness. drink not to elation.
–BENJAMIN FRANKLIN

Eat with the rich, but go to play with the poor.
–LOGAN P. SMITH

Enough is as good as a feast.
–JOHN HEYWOOD

Everything in the world may be endured except continual prosperity.
–JOHANN VON GOETHE

Every shut eye ain't asleep.
–BLACK AMERICAN

Fool me once, shame on you; fool me twice, shame on me.
–ORIENT

Force is not a remedy.
–JOHN BRIGHT

For one word a man is often thought to be wise, and for one word he is often thought to be foolish. We ought to be careful indeed what we say.
–CONFUCIUS

Fear makes the wolf bigger than he is.
–GERMAN

. . .For want of a nail the shoe was lost;
for want of a shoe the horse was lost;
and for want of a horse the rider was lost.
–GEORGE HERBERT

Fine words butter no parsnips.
–SOUTH AMERICAN

Fear less, hope more; eat less, chew more; whine less,

breathe more, talk less, say more; hate less, love more; And all good things are yours.
—SWEDISH

God has given you one face, and you make yourself another.
—ORIENT

Gray hair is a sign of age, not of wisdom.
— GREEK

God gave man two eyes and two ears and one mouth to the end that he would see and hear more than he speaks.
—SOCRATES

Grief can take care of itself, but to get the full value of a joy you must have somebody to divide it with.
—MARK TWAIN

He gives nothing who gives not of himself.
—FRENCH

He who sleeps in continual noise is awakened by silence.
—HOWELLS

He who would bring home the wealth of the Indies, must carry the wealth of the Indies with him.
—SPANISH

Happiness is something you may have for just a day, As you can never keep it if you don't give it away.
—THELMA IRELAND

He who sees the dawn, gets the herring.
—IRISH

Habits are at first cobwebs—then cables.
—SPANISH

He who has seen the light, doesn't tolerate the dark very

long.
—ENGLISH

Help thy brother's boat across, and lo! Thine own has
reached the shore.
—HINDU

He who sings frightens away his ills.
—SPANISH

He saith little that loveth much.
—ITALIAN

He is happiest, be he king or peasant, who finds peace in
his home.
—JOHANN VON GOETHE

He who chases two rabbits won't catch either one.
—CZECHOSLOVAK

Happiness is a butterfly, which when pursued, is always
just beyond your grasp, but which, if you will sit down quietly
may alight upon you.
—NATHANIEL HAWTHORNE

He who limps is still walking.
—SWISS

He who fears death enjoys not life.
—SPANISH

Having a good wife and rich cabbage soup, seek not other
things.
—RUSSIAN

If a man combats a wave it overpowers him.
If he permits it to roll over him, the wave passes on.
—THE TALMUD

I wake to sleep, and take my walking slow. I learn by going where I have to go.
—THEODORE ROETHKE

If fifty million people saw a foolish thing, it is still a foolish thing.
—ANATOLE FRANCE

If I had but two loaves of bread, I would sell one and buy hyacinth, for they would feed my soul.
—VERSE OF KORAN

If you seek a pleasant peninsula, look around you.
—ENGLISH

I wept when I was born and every day explains why.
—SPANISH

If I keep a green bough in my heart, the singing bird will come.
—CHINESE

In a shop, courtesy and quality go hand in hand.
—TUNNARD

If I listen, I have the advantage. If I speak, others have.
—ARABIC

It is better for a woman to marry a man who loves her, than a man she loves.
—ARABIC

If you want to be happy for a few hours, get drunk;
If you want to be happy for a week-end, get   married;
If you want to be happy for a whole week, barbecue a pig—
And if you want to be happy for a life time, become a gardener.
—ORIENT

It is easier to be wise for others than for ourselves.
—LA ROCHEFOUCAULD

If you would know the value of money, go out and try to borrow some.
—BENJAMIN FRANKLIN

It is better to be stupid like everyone than to be clever like no one.
—ANATOLE FRANCE

If two people are together, it's a festival.
—BASQUE

If you cannot sing, you die.
—SIBERIAN

It is better to be hated for what you are than to be loved for what you are not.
—ANDRE GIDE

If you go to war, pray once; if you go on a sea journey, pray twice; but pray three times when you are going to be married.
—RUSSIAN

It is no use to wait for your ship to come in unless you have sent one out.
—BELGIAN

If you're late, don't hurry. You're already late.
—ALGONKIAN

Know thyself. . . .and nothing to excess.
—SOCRATES

Knowledge comes by taking things apart—
Wisdom by putting things together.
—DANISH

Know your limits and where you are, if you want to get where you are going.
—ITALIAN

Know the true value of time. Snatch, seize and enjoy every moment of it.
—LORD CHESTERFIELD

Keep quiet, and people will think you are a philosopher.
—LATIN

Keep your eyes wide open before marriage, half shut afterwards.
—BENJAMIN FRANKLIN

Let me never condem my brother until I have walked sun-up to sun-down in his moccasins.
—INDIAN

Love your neighbour—yet pull not down the hedge.
—GEORGE HERBERT

Light is the task when many share the toil.
—HOMER

Laziness travels so slowly that poverty soon overtakes him.
—BENJAMIN FRANKLIN

Let thy discontents be secrets.
—BENJAMIN FRANKLIN

Many toil hard to earn a loaf when a slice is sufficient.
—DUTCH

Men learn little from victory, but much from defeat.
—ENGLISH

Misfortunes always come in by a door that has been left open to them.
—CZECHOSLOVAK

May happiness, like trade winds, awake thee.
—ALOHA GREETING

Make not a fence more expensive or more important than the thing that is fenced.
—HEBREW

Not the load—but the overload that kills.
—SPANISH

Never give advice in a crowd.
—ARABIAN

Not all good comes to any man.
—PERSIAN

Never let the sun set without having enjoyed a sprig of parsley.
—GERMAN

Needles and pins, needles and pins. When you get married your trouble begins.
—OLD NURSERY RHYME

No one of you is a believer until he loves for his brother what he loves for himself.
—ISLAM

Not to decide is to decide.
—MONTEREY

Nothing fixes a thing so intensely in the memory as the wish to forget it.
—MONTAIGNE

No human creature can give orders to love.
—GEORGE SAND

Never throw anyone so far away you can't reach him.
—ENGLISH

One thing about telling the truth—you don't need a good memory.
—ABRAHAM LINCOLN

On the day of victory, no one is tired.
—ARABIC

Of soup and love the first is the best.
—SPANISH

One pound of learning requires 150 pounds of common sense to apply it.
—PERSIAN

Peace comes from within. Do not seek it without.
—BUDDHA

Poor man, said I, you pay too much for your whistle.
—BENJAMIN FRANKLIN

Pleasure is often spoiled by describing it.
—HENRI STENDHAL

Proverbs bear age; and he who would do well may view himself in them as in a looking glass.
—ITALIAN

Sweet are the thoughts that savour of content; The quiet mind is richer than a crown.
—ROBERT GREENE

Some die too young, and some die too old; The precept sounds strange, but die at the right time.
—FRIEDRICH NIETZCHE

Sometimes you have to be silent to be heard.
—SWISS

To go slowly and to live a long time are two brothers.
—DUTCH

To a quick question, give a slow answer.
—NORWEGIAN

The strongest memory is weaker than the palest ink.
—ORIENT

The journey of one thousand miles begins with a single step.
—CHINESE

To be able to look back upon one's life with satisfaction is to live twice.
—HORACE

To teach is to learn twice.
—ORIENT

To be content with what we possess is the greatest and most secure of riches.
—CICERO

The girl who can't dance says the band can't play.
—YIDDISH

Terrifying are the weaknesses of power.
—GREEK

To enjoy life, we must touch much of it lightly.
—VOLTAIRE

There's a time to wink as well as to see.
—BENJAMIN FRANKLIN

Treat your friend as if he might become an enemy.
—PUBLIUS SYRUS

The greater the difficulty, the greater the glory.
—CICERO

The early morning hours have gold in their hand.
—SWEDISH

The Gods do not subtract from the allotted span of men's lives the hours spent in fishing.
—ASSYRIAN TABLET OF 2000 B. C.

The more help a man has in his garden, the less it belongs to him.
—W. H. DAVIES

The grand essentials in this life are:
something to do, something to love, and something to hope for.
—JOSEPH ADDISON

The braver the bird, the fatter the cat.
—HEBREW

Wealth is not his who has it, but his who enjoys it.
—CHINESE

Who gives to me teaches me to give.
—DUTCH

We are shrewder at sunrise than at moonrise.
—RUSSIAN

With money in your pocket, you are wise, and you are handsome, and you can sing well, too.
—YIDDISH

We grow too soon old and too late smart.
—DUTCH

In the Indian family the grandfather played a most important role; he taught the children integrity, a code of morals, and a

respect for human individuality.
—FREDDA DUDLEY BALLING

Learning adds to the brightness of one's countenance;
Learning is wealth secured beyond all risk;
Learning is fundamental to world peace.
—SANSKRIT POEM OF ANCIENT INDIA

Open hearts of the listening ones, that the words which
you shall give me may enter therein, and dwell for all times;
that we might walk together as brothers, and know one another
with an understanding heart.
—NIPO STRONGHEART

There is no one luckier than he who thinks himself so.
—GERMAN

The hungry man does not hear.
—SWAHILI

Wealth in cattle, wealth in elephants, wealth in gold,
wealth in gems—all are as dust when wealth in contentment
comes.
—HINDU

We may delay but time will not.
—BENJAMIN FRANKLIN

Wouldst thou know if a people be well governed, its laws
be good or bad?   Examine the music it practices.
—CONFUCIUS

We must get rid of the extraordinary notion that manual
work is degrading.
—JAWAHARAL NEHRU

We wish to you. . . .
         deep peace of the running wave;
         deep peace of the flowing air;

deep peace of the quiet earth;
deep peace of the shining star—
To you.
—THE OLD BLESSING OF ST. COLUMBO

Do not insult the mother alligator until after you have crossed the river.
—HAITIAN

He that hath no brother hath weak legs.
—PERSIAN

It is always a silly thing to give advice, but to give good advice is absolutely fatal.
—OSCAR WILDE

Unless men travel the same road together, they cannot sit down and talk together.
—CONFUCIUS

EDUCATION

A changing society may be part of the student unrest and his not working up to his potential. Doing well in school may not be valued as highly by young people and parents as it once was. In an age of calculators and computers, reading, writing and arithmetic may not seem as essential as they once did.
—DR. LESTER ELIJAH

Accept your child for what he is—not for what you want him to be.
—DR. PAUL HANNA

All children have the ability to create.
—BARBARA KEYES

Always be on the side of the child.
—JACK SHORE

As we read the school reports on our children we realize with a sense of relief that—thank Heaven—nobody is reporting in this fashion on us.
—J. B. PRIESTLEY

Ain't it funny, teacher? I was just thinking the same thing about you.
—JOHNNY JONES
> (Johnny was kept in after school for misbehaviour. He and his teacher worked quietly at their desks. Afterwards, Johnny cleaned the erasers. Things were so friendly, the teacher asked Johnny why he couldn't be nice like this during class time).

Accountability should be to the kids. Not to the administration, or the school board members, or to the taxpayers.
—MARTY WILSON

As teachers, some of us tend to be keepers of the class, rather than curators of the mind.
—LLOYD W. KLINE

A child's success depends a lot more on what kind of a home he comes from--than what kind of a school he goes to.
—ERIC SEVAREID

At least seventy-five percent of all children in public schools today were entered into kindergarten too young.
—DR. FRANCES ILG

Always be kind to your A and B students. Someday one of them will return to your campus as a professor. And also be kind to your C students. Someday one of them will build you a two million dollar science laboratory.
—HAROLD A. FITZGERALD

A child acts according to the environment he hears.
—THELMA McAFEE

All children need love —especially when they don't deserve it.
—HAROLD S. HULBERT

A teacher's mental health is more contagious than the measles.
—DR. WILLIAM MENNINGER

A teacher who can arouse a feeling for one single good action, for one single good poem, accomplishes more than he who fills our memory with rows on rows of natural objects, classified with name and form.
—JOHANN VON GOETHE

A child remembers a loving parent. He forgets a dirty kitchen.
—ALTON BLAKESLEE

A kid who can't learn to read stands naked before the world.
—JENKIN LLOYD JONES

A man's immortality comes from those whom he teaches.
—ANDREN SEGOVIA

Being a parent is the hardest job in the world. It's up-hill all the way. But maybe it's the most important job in the world.
—GRACE KELLY

Basically, children are inquisitive and curious and really want to go to school to learn about their world, and get answers to their questions.
—DR. FRITZ WENDT

Better the father who roars than the father who shrugs.
—DR. DONALD BARR

Children have different learning styles. They have different rhythms, and so should be treated differently.
—ARDEN THORUN

Children owe their parents nothing. The parents are simply paying off their debt to society by rearing and taking care of their children.
—JOHN TYLER

Catch your children being good.
—DR. SHEILA EYBERG

Call the new fads in education an innovation if you want to—but they're really just ideas from the little old red school-house.
—DR. VIRGIL HOLLIS

Children have more need of models than of critics.
—JOSEPH JOUBERT

Child rearing should be fun—at least fifty-percent of the time—or parents should get out of the business.
—DR. LENDON SMITH

141

Chronological age is the poorest indicator of what a child can do.
–JIM HARRELL

Discipline is the strongest support a student has.
–DR. DONALD BARR

Do we have to do what we want to do today, teacher?
–BILLY SCHULTZ

Experience be a jewel that I have purchased at an infinite rate.
–WILLIAM SHAKESPEARE

Education unbinds the mind.
–AMISH

Educational processes–as well as governmental–should be out in the open. It's amazing how fine a person can be when he is sitting out on the front porch.
–JOHN GARDNER

Education is the ability to listen to almost anything without losing your temper or your self-confidence.
–ROBERT FROST

Education is that which remains when one has forgotten everything he has learned in school.
–ALBERT EINSTEIN

Education should not be a destination, but a road we travel all the days of our lives.
–ORVILLE C. PRATT

Examples set at home count more than any lectures at school.
–JUDY STRANGIS

Everyone's out of step but John.
–JOHN'S MOTHER

Education is. . .hanging around until you've caught on.
—ROBERT FROST

From conception on, child-bearing is geared to getting the child out of the house. If you're getting along beautifully with your teen-age son, you just may have a forty-year old son still around when you're sixty.
—DR. LENDON SMITH

Give a little love to a child, and you get a great deal back.
—JOHN RUSKIN

How green I was my first year of teaching! My principal told me to be in charge of the ball-room. My first thoughts were of the schottische, the polka, the hardwood floors—he took me to a room of baseballs, basketballs and footballs.
—MARTINE CAMPBELL

How do I know what I want to be when I grow up? Maybe they haven't even invented my job yet.
—PAUL HASTINGS

How children feel about things is more important than what they know about things.
—DANIEL FISCHER

He who can, does. He who cannot, teaches.
—GEORGE BERNARD SHAW

History to most pupils means names, places, and dates. Only a good teacher can make it clear that history is really a study of change, process, and development.
—SYDNEY J. HARRIS

I only have one friend, and I hate him.
—MARVIN JOHNSON, 2nd GRADER

I'd like a teacher that's not afraid to laugh with you, and never thinks of laughing at you.
—WALLY POTTER

143

If we let them, children can lead us—like Pied Piper in reverse—back to the bright world of spontaneity and wonder that we thought we had lost forever.
—EDA J. LESHAN

I wish I could remember that new word I learned yesterday.
—MIKE OTTO

I don't learn because my teacher does not expect me to.
—JOHNNY JOHNSTON

I can take people in their fifties and sixties and whip them into shape in six weeks. These are the people who walked to school. For teen-agers, it takes two years to accomplish as much. They have never built a body. Schools bussed them to and from. They have been pampered.
—RUTH CARLTON

If you want to find out what children can do, you have to stop giving them things.
—NORMAN DOUGLAS

I've got a friend I haven't even met yet.
—BRUCE SCOTT, 2nd GRADER

If parents would only realize how they bore their children!
—GEORGE BERNARD SHAW

If there is such a thing as a touchstone in education, it is this belief in the dignity of the individual as a human being.
—ANGELO GIAUDRONE

I am not an under-achiever. My teacher is an over-expecter.
—BEN KNAPP

I'll work wherever my country needs me. What work it is is not important.
—A CHINESE CHILD

It is a great thing to start life with a small number of really

good books that are your very own.
—ARTHUR CONAN DOYLE

I never let schooling interfere with my education.
—MARK TWAIN

I was a strict teacher. I always held that no school room
was big enough for an unruly child.
—MISS ELEANOR
(President Carter's First grade teacher)

It has always astounded me that the only job we tackle without any real previous training is that of being a parent.
—DR. WILLIAM TUTTLE

The hardest thing about teaching is the motivation. If
anyone can figure that out, education's got it made.
—CHARLTON HESTON

In education we are striving not to teach youth to make a
living, but to make a life.
— WILLIAM ALLEN WHITE

In my first twenty-five years of teaching, I had at least
forty-five children in my class. But I didn't realize I had too
many students, because no one had ever told me so.
—GRACE THORNDYKE

If a teacher sets himself above a student, he will be met
with a like response from the student, and little communication
will result.
—ROBERT W. TORMEY

I used to drive a school bus, but I couldn't stand the noise.
—ONE JACKHAMMER OPERATOR TO ANOTHER

It's up to the kid to do some of the work instead of saying,
"Feed me."
—KATHARINE HEPBURN

I'm supposed to use the big stick in my office. But I don't have one. I have a cookie jar instead.
—JACK SHORE, PRINCIPAL

I am always ready to learn, but I do not always like being taught.
—SIR WINSTON CHURCHILL

I am weary of people who say that music is a frill of education. Music is the very core of our society.
—MILTON KATIMS

I think the community colleges are the greatest thing since peanut butter.
—DRU BRIGGS

I taught anyone who wanted to learn anything I could teach him.
—BOOKER T. WASHINGTON

I have to meet the child where he is—he doesn't have to come to meet me.
—ALICE O'NEIL

If I do little else, I want to send my students away with at least as much interest in the subject I teach, as they had when they arrived.
—ROBERT F. MAGER

It is my theory that if you have one good teacher all the time you are going to school, you are lucky. I was real lucky. I had two.
—FRANK McGEE

I've been a remedial reading teacher for so long that when I visited the Capital of Arizona I wrote my address from Phonics, Arizona.
—BEULAH BURNS

I have often reflected the new vistas that reading opened to me. I knew right there in prison that reading had changed forever the course of my life.
—MALCOLM X

It only hurts when I laugh.
—DANNY BENDER

I've got my own dogs to chase.
—CELIA ATWOOD
    (on letting her children grow up)

I study very hard. I learn English. But Marines not talk same.
—SMALL VIETNAMESE BOY

I've got to like him. He's the only friend I've got.
—MATT TAYLOR

I try to push the student into an intellectual corner, and I let him fight it out.
—ROBERT A. HORN

I know you're disappointed in me, Dad, but why aren't you ever appointed in me?
—SCOTT JONES

I can give you explanations but I cannot give you understanding.
—JOHN HUNGATE

If there is any national religion in our country, it is education.
—ERIC SEVAREID

I love teaching at the state penetentiary. I deal with men on an adult basis, and there are no recess duties, no bulletin boards, and no PTA meetings.
—JOHN BUTLER

I find my fulfillment not in, "I can teach you," but in, "You can learn."
—ROBERT HEYER

Kids are great until they're 12.
—JACK SHORE

Look kids right in the eye. Then say, "What you expect of me, I expect of myself."
—DR. JO STANCHFIELD

Love children into learning.
—DR. JO STANCHFIELD

Let's begin to insist that children be children for the very short years of childhood, and put the Red Queen back into the storybook, where she belongs.
—JOYCE KISSOCK LUBOLD

Many women and men are magnificently unsuited to be parents.
—DR. MARGARET MEAD

Man without education is like marble in a quarry.
—JOSEPH ADDISON

Most of us are too concerned with what our children are doing. We should be more concerned about what our children are being.
—SYDNEY J. SMITH

No man has completed his education who has not learned to live with an unsoluble problem.
—EDMUND J. KIEFER

No difference will be made unless we reach the classroom.
—RUTH HOLLOWAY

Now I must learn to let you walk alone. Withdraw the mentor's hand before it turns to weight that you must carry

and bemoan.
—LOIS PAULSEN

No one can misunderstand a boy like his own mother.
—NORMAN DOUGLAS

Not only is Johnny the worst behaved child in school; he
also has a perfect attendance record.
—FRANCES ANDREWS

Nothing improves a composition more than the red pencil.
—LEO TOLSTOI

No one ever keeps a secret so well as a child.
—VICTOR HUGO

No matter how happy one's adult life is, the unmet needs of
childhood linger on, doling out remembered pain on a regular
basis.
—CLORIS LEACHMAN

One father is more than a hundred school masters.
—GEORGE HERBERT

One of the most misleading phrases in modern society is
"compulsory education"; it is impossible to have compulsory
education—the most you can achieve is compulsory attendance.
—SYDNEY J. HARRIS

Our schools should stop concentrating on teaching the
children so much knowledge, and start teaching them a little
wisdom.
—WESLEY TAYLOR

Only parents' love can last our lives.
—ROBERT BROWNING

Reading should be for children an integral part of life,
like eating, and loving, and playing.
—CLIFTON FADIMAN

School is a building that has four walls—with tomorrow inside.
—LON WALTERS

School days, I believe, are the unhappiest in the whole span of human existence.
—H. L. MENCKEN

There is no education like adversity.
—BENJAMIN DISRAELI

The magic of learning is not in the schools, not in the tools, but in the child.
—DR. NEIL CAYS

The worse a child is, the more understanding he needs.
—DR. LILLIAN GRAY

The most necessary task of civilization is to teach man how to think.
—RALPH WALDO EMERSON

The first half of our lives is ruined by our parents, and the second half by our children.
—CLARENCE DARROW

The fundamental defect of fathers is that they want their children to be a credit to them.
—BERTRAND RUSSELL

There are three classes of people in the world—men, women, and schoolteachers.
—ELMER KIBBEE

The teacher should spend half her time learning her children, and the other half teaching them.
—DORIS BOSWORTH

The schoolmaster is abroad, and I trust to him, armed with his primer, against the soldier in full military array.
—HENRY PETER

Teaching disadvantaged children may make Christians out of us all.
–DR. JO STANCHFIELD

The teacher places his signature on his work, just as truly as the painter who writes his in the lower corner of his painting.
–ERNEST L. MELBY

The early reader is a pencil and paper kid.
–DR. JOYCE BROTHERS

The child who figures out how the pencil sharpener works is often graded lower than the child who keeps his pencils sharpened.
–ARLENE SILBERMAN

Teaching all of the children of all of the people is as exciting as working with nuclear physics.
–MARY C. AUSTIN

The best way to train a child in the way he should go, is to travel that road occasionally yourself.
–JOSH BILLINGS

The parents' life is the child's copybook.
–GIBSON

The word childhood used to conjure up a pleasant picture of long, lazy days and amusing episodes of mischief. Today every parent knows that after school there must be enrich-ment in the form of music lessons, or sports. There are no long, lazy days any more.
–JOYCE KISSOCK LUBOLD

The pupil who is never required to do what he cannot do, never does what he can do.
–JOHN STUART MILL

To know how to grow old is the master work of wisdom,

and one of the most difficult chapters in the great art of living.
–HENRI FREDERIC AMIEL

We need grandmothers a lot more than we need experts.
–DR. L. F. ATWOOD

When you talk to the parents, you can tell if you want their son on your football team.
–COACH JIM SWEENEY

We are raising a 'gimme' generation. By giving, we must teach children not just to take, but to give in return.
–DR. ERIKA FREEMAN

When grandparents enter the door, discipline flies out the window.
–OGDEN NASH

We must crawl before we read. A baby develops his tacility as he brushes with the floor. He develops his depth perception as he measures distances of his journey. He acquires balance. But, above all, he is developing one of the vital layers of his brain.
–DR. ROBERT MORRIS

We have to teach our child to walk—and then, to walk away.
–DR. SONYA FRIEDMAN

When children mature earlier, they rebel earlier.
–HARRIET VAN HORNE

What is the first part of politics? Education. The second? Education. And the third? Education.
–JULES MICHELET

We gave our children everything—we gave them our time.
–ROBERT AND CLARISSA HANSEN

When you have to get the attention of a room full of noisy

elementary school children, you've got to surprise them. I walk in the room with a plastic face pinned on my tie. I pull a string to make his nose light up. Sometimes I stand on a folding chair, raise my pant cuffs to expose a bright orange stocking—and sometimes I play on my dulcimer. Quiet? You can hear a pin drop!
—WILSON BUNDY

When you give your child a bath, bathe him in language.
—JOHN CHANCELLOR

Worst thing we ever did was close the country schools. The children there really learned. And there was discipline. They didn't mess around at school because they knew the teacher wouldn't stand for it and their folks wouldn't, either.
—ALICE WILLARD

We learn more about ourselves by watching children.
—ALEXANDRA STODDARD

When we adults want to enjoy ourselves, we almost always seek to be entertained by others—when a child plays, he lets his imagination transform the commonplace into the priceless.
—EDA J. LE SHAN

We can neither produce it—hurry it—nor ignore it. When a child is ready he will: be born—walk—talk—read.
—JIM HARRELL

We can't teach children until we reach children.
—RUSSELL KIRK

We go to school to everyone we meet.
—DR. PAUL HANNA

We should not ask if children are successful in school, but are schools successful with our children?
—DR. WILTON M. KROGMAN

We have five bowels: a,e,i,o, and u.
—JOE TANNER, 2nd GRADER

When it comes to success as a highschool student, the earlies have it.
–MARTY WILSON

When ulcers forced me out of my landscape engineering, I went back to college at age forty-seven to obtain teaching credentials. I was fifty when I began teaching. I always felt that somewhere along the line there was room for me to give something. And I found it, in the classroom.
–CARL BRODEN

Your folks had to take you, but I was picked out.
–ADOPTED BOY, ROY DAVIS

Young people–the majority of young people–want to do something worth while. They are idealistic and feel that they can make a difference.
–MARLO THOMAS

You cannot teach a man anything; you can only help him find it out for himself.
–GALILEO GALILEI

Youngsters in my third grade class aren't wasting their free time on childish mischief–they're too busy playing chess. As soon as they come in to school in the morning, it's straight to the chess boards.
–CARTER COATES

You see many people out exercising their dog–when they should be out exercising their child.
–DR. NATHAN SMITH

Youth is wholly experimental.
–ROBERT LOUIS STEVENSON

Begin where it starts.
–DR. JO STANCHFIELD

Children need a good self-image to cope with the world. All of them must be winners at something.
–DR. LENDON SMITH

One might say education is not to make anything of anybody, but simply to open the minds of everyone–to go from cocksure ignorance to thoughtful uncertainty.
–EUGENE P. BERTIN

School is like a tailor that fits the boy to the pants, not the pants to the boy.
–DR. FRANCES ILG

Some children will not be able to improve in school work until certain conditions in their homelife have been changed.
–DENNIS GALLAGHER

The important thing is that the child knows he's being listened to. His problems are not just his. His problems are being understood by others.
–PEGGY MANN

When the young behave badly, it is because society has already behaved worse.
–J. B. PRIESTLEY

Your children may turn out all right after all.
–DR. ERIKA FREEMAN

Children are our most valuable natural resource.
–HERBERT HOOVER

Education is an admirable thing. but it is well to remember from time to time that nothing that is worth knowing can be taught.
–OSCAR WILDE

Fiddlers three? Dad, don't you mean a three piece string combo?
–REAMER KELLER

Miss Eleanor. Tomorrow I'll bring you my mother's diamond ring. Daddy can get her another one.
—JIMMY CARTER
(a first grader speaks to his teacher)

Oh, sure, I worry about my report card, but I worry more about creating a good image.
—TOMMY JONES, 5th GRADER

To learn something new, take the path that you took yesterday.
—JOHN BURROUGHS

RELIGION

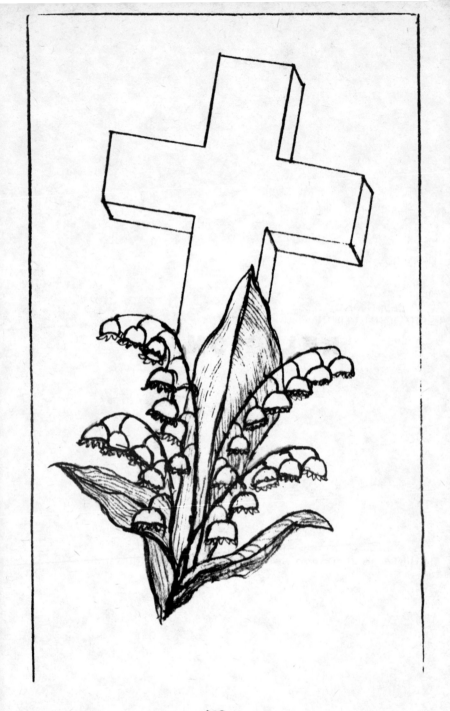

A watch cannot be made without a watchmaker, any more than the universe can be made without a universe maker.
–HUBERT HUMPHREY

And with all the needy, O divide, I pray. This vast treasure of content that is mine today.
–JAMES WHITCOMB RILEY

An honest man's the noblest work of God.
–ALEXANDER POPE

All religions must be tolerated, for every man must get to Heaven in his own way.
–FREDERICK THE GREAT

A happy family is but an earlier heaven.
–SIR JOHN BOWRING

A person is closer to God when he's in his garden. His mental anxieties are erased. His animosities disappear.
–JERRY BAKER

At the close of life the question will not be how much have you got, but how much have you given; not how much were you honored, but how much have you served.
–NATHAN C. SCHAEFFER

A verse may find him who a sermon flies.
–GEORGE HERBERT

As the clay to the potter, as the windmill to the wind, as children to their sire, we beseech of Thee this help and mercy for Christ's sake.
–ROBERT LOUIS STEVENSON

All good drama is religious. If it tells the truth about life and the human heart, if it speaks of men's failings and also their grandeur and hope, then it's religious. That's my idea of religion–dealing honestly with life.
–JULIE HARRIS

A truly religious person will be willing to walk the second mile.
—ORAL ROBERTS

At New Year's time, I don't want confetti streaming down my throat nor the noise with all the trimmings. I love the peace and quiet and knowing God has given me another day that could stretch out as long as a year. This is the New Year for me.
—PEARL BAILEY

As one may ascend to the housetop by ladder, rope, or bamboo, so there are many ways to reach God.
—FROM THE HINDU

A prayer spoken by an old mountain man that might apply to all of us, flatlanders and hill people alike:

Lord, I don't ask for a faith that would move yonder mountain. I can take enough dynamite and move it, if it needs movin'. I pray, Lord, for enough faith to move me.
—NORMAN ALLEN

A religion that does nothing, that gives nothing, that costs nothing, is worth nothing.
—L. D. MOODY

All that which pleases is but for a moment. That only is important which is eternal.
—OVER THE GREAT DOORS OF MILAN CATHEDRAL

And if, in time of sacred youth, we learned at home to Love and Pray,
Pray Heaven that early Love and Truth may never wholly pass away.
—WILLIAM THACKERAY

As a very young child, I was taught never to use the word 'you' or 'your' when referring to God. The word was too

commonplace. We should, instead, use Thee and Thou. To this day, fifty years later, I cringe to the core when I hear even very renown pastors say something like, "You know what is in my heart, O God."
—ORA B. LANDIS

By the thousands, kids today have discovered Jesus. It is a pity that when they were small and went to church He wasn't made real to them. They found people just going through the motions, and because they put very little into it, they got very little out of it. Now Jesus is back, because kids are personally feeling His power.
—NORMAN VINCENT PEALE

Be as Christian as you seem and seem as Christian as you are.
—HARRY EMERSON FOSDICK

But it is now time to depart, for me to die, for you to live. But which of us is going to a better state is unknown to every one but God.
—SOCRATES

Because of our traditions, everyone knows who he is and what God expects of him.
—SHOLEM ALEICHEM

But Heaven holds all for which you sigh—There! little girl; don't cry.
—JAMES WHITCOMB RILEY

Count you many blessings, count them one by one; and it will surprise you what the Lord hath done.
—OLD CHURCH HYMN

Do what lieth in thy power, and God will assist thy good will.
—THOMAS A. KEMPIS

Deep in the forest or far out at sea, God is where we want

Him to be.
—GENEVIEVE YOUNG

Everyone has at least one sermon in him.
—BOB SNYDER

Every man's life is a fairy tale written by God's fingers.
—HANS CHRISTIAN ANDERSEN

Every religion teaches we're entitled to another chance.
—DR. MAXWELL MALTZ

Everyone should live from his heart and make a joyful noise unto the Lord. Then he won't need stimulants. Spiritual values will give him all the strength he needs.
—LIONEL HAMPTON

Everybody wants to go to Heaven, but nobody wants to die.
—JOE LOUIS

For when the One Great Scorer comes to write against your name, he marks—not that you won or lost—But how you played the game.
—GRANTLAND RICE

Faith in an all-seeing personal God, elevates the soul, purifies the emotions, sustains human dignity, and lends poetry, nobility and holiness to the commonest state, and manner of life.
—JUAN VALERA

For the Christ-Child who comes is the Master of all; no palace too great, no cottage too small.
—PHILLIPS BROOKS

For frantic boast and foolish word—Thy mercy on Thy People, Lord!
—RUDYARD KIPLING

Four things a man must learn to do

If he would make his record true:
To think without confusion clearly;
To love his fellow men sincerely;
To act from honest motives purely;
To trust in God and Heaven securely.
—HENRY VAN DYKE

Follow your compass and trust in God.
—GARY SCHNEIDER
(when lost sixteen days on Mt. Hood)

God cares for trees but any fool can destroy them.
—JOHN MUIR

God did not play tricks on us. He gave us brains to
understand the mysteries of the Universe.
—GALILEO

God doth not need either man's work, or His own gifts;
Who best bear His mild yoke, they serve Him best.
—JOHN MILTON

God's in His Heaven
All's right with the world!
—ROBERT BROWNING

God and hard work are the best doctors.
—JOHN MUIR

Going to church doesn't make you a Christian any more
than going to a garage makes you an automobile.
—W. A. "BILLY" SUNDAY

God! Clean my heart, lift my mind, and make me my
brother's brother.
—ARTHUR S. FREESE

Give me a great task and then when I'm through, God leave
me almost always with something to do.
—BETTY YOUNG

God, give us courage and gaiety and the quiet mind.
—ROBERT LOUIS STEVENSON

God has to nearly kill us sometimes to teach us lessons.
—JOHN MUIR

Go to sleep; God is awake.
—VICTOR HUGO

God has much to say to those who will listen.
—M. E. MIDDLEMASS

God be thanked for books. They are the voices of the distant and the dead, and make us heirs of the spiritual life of the past ages. Books are the true levelers.
—WILLIAM CHANNING

God obligeth no man to more than He hath given him to perform.
—THE KORAN

Going up in a balloon is the closest you can get to God and nature. For one thing, you are praying all the time.
—ROD McKUEN

God will not look you over for medals, degrees, or diplomas, but for scars.
—ELBERT HUBBARD

God has given us tongues that we may say something pleasant to our fellow-men.
—HEINRICH HEINE

God moves in a mysterious way. His wonders to perform.
—WILLIAM COWPER

God knows, I'm not the thing I should be, nor am I even the thing I could be.
—ROBERT BURNS

God gave us memories so that we would have roses in December.
—SIR JAMES BARRIE

God has given us two hands—one to receive with and the other to give with.
—BILLY GRAHAM

God give me sympathy and sense,
And keep my courage high;
God, give me calm and confidence,
And please. . .A twinkle in my eye.
—A TEACHER'S PRAYER

God's finger touched him, and he slept.
—ALFRED TENNYSON

God always answers prayers. Sometimes He says, "Yes." Sometimes He says, "No." Sometimes He says, "Wait a while."
—ORA LANDIS

God is and all is well.
—JOHN GREENLEAF WHITTIER

God is in me or else is not at all.
—WALLACE STEVENS

God, give us grace—each in his place
To bear his lot,
And murmuring not, endure and wait and labor.
—MARTIN LUTHER

God makes rainy days as well as sunny days. A rainy day is not bad. God makes everything good—real good.
—TAXI DRIVER IN NEW YORK

Give God time.
—THE KORAN

Heaven is above all yet; there is a judge that no king can corrupt.
—WILLIAM SHAKESPEARE

I like it here where the hawthorns grow,
Where silence speaks of eternal things,
And deep within me my heart sings.
—PENNY ANDERSON

I believe in a spiritual world and I believe we're living in it now. God is different for different people and if we have any chance at peace in this world, it's each one of us working out our relationship with God.
—DORIS DAY

I say the whole earth and all the stars in the sky are for religion's sake.
—WALT WHITMAN

If God seems far away, look around you. God is everywhere, and in each one of us.
—REV. GEORGE W. SWANK

I sought to hear the voice of God,
And climbed the topmost steeple.
But God declared: Go down again,
I dwell among the people.
—LOUIS I. NEWMAN

I shall hear music in Heaven.
—MOZART

I myself believe that the evidence for God lies primarily in inner personal experiences.
—WILLIAM JAMES

I don't believe God was that stupid—to create a person who grows and grows—in both mind and body—and then lets him fall apart later on. No, I'm not an old lady, ready to be put on the shelf.
—ADELA ROGERS ST. JOHN

Into every man's life comes a glimpse of the eternal.
—JAMES HILTON

I don't recall much of the sermon that day, because I was too busy watching a sermon out the window.
—BUDDY NEFF

If thou follow but thy star, thou cans't not miss at last a glorious Haven.
—ALIGHIERI DANTE

I think in every person there is something that is beneficial—if we can get that good to come out. We need a system that really takes note of the presence of God in every human being.
—DR. GEORGE HALL

I thank God for my handicaps, for through them I have found myself, my work, and my God.
—HELEN KELLER

I don't know if Jesus Christ laughed or not, but he sure made it possible for me to laugh.
—REV. J. H. JAHR

I went down to my knees in prayer, because I had the profound conviction I had no where else to go.
—ABRAHAM LINCOLN

If you don't have any problems, you should get down on your knees and pray, "What's the matter, Lord, don't you trust me with a problem?"
—DR. NORMAN VINCENT PEALE

It is not when I am going to meet Him, but when I am just turning away and leaving Him, that I discover that God is.
—HENRY DAVID THOREAU

I'd rather see a sermon than hear one any day,

I'd rather one should walk with me
Than merely tell the way.
–EDGAR ALBERT GUEST

I never spoke with God, nor visited in Heaven—Yet
certain am I of the spot as if the Checks were given.
–EMILY DICKINSON

I like the silent church before the service begins, better
than any preaching.
–RALPH WALDO EMERSON

Isn't God upon the ocean, just the same as on the land?
–JAMES THOMAS FIELDS

I hope to see my Pilot face to face when I have crossed
the bar.
–ALFRED TENNYSON

I lost my money and saved my soul.
–DR. ALBERT SZENT-GYORGYI

I'm a very religious man. Not denominationally—but deep
inside. I'm on earth to take care of some things here. And
God's on earth to take care of things there.
–HUBERT HUMPHREY

I believe in life after death. It would all be so purposeless
otherwise. We sleep one-third of our life away. Think of all
the time we spend in the minutiae of life. . .brushing teeth—
combing hair—getting dressed. What have we learned? I
can't believe that's all there is.
–GLORIA SWANSON

I never behold the Heavens that I do not feel that I am
looking in the face of God. I can see how it might be possible
for a man to look down upon the earth and become an atheist,
but I cannot conceive how he could look up into the Heavens
and say there is no God.
–ABRAHAM LINCOLN

168

If there is only one God, then all people be brothers.
—PASTOR DON ROGNE

I thank God for letting her touch my life.
—SAMMY DAVIS JR.
(speaking of Mahalia Jackson)

I didn't go to no school to learn how to preach. I got my training from God.
—MOTHER ELIZABETH BAKER, PASTOR

In the beginning God created everything, and then he set it to music.
—PATRICIA J. OUGHTON

If God wanted to be loved as well as feared, He moved correctly—to have His Son come in the form of a helpless baby.
—HARRY REASONER

If God made the world in seven days, He must have made man late Saturday night when He was tired.
—MARK TWAIN

It is amazing the number of people who have an individual concept of God.
—DR. GEORGE HALL

If there's room in God's garden for weeds, there's room in mine.
—JERRY BAKER

If men are so wicked with religion, what would they be without it?
—BENJAMIN FRANKLIN

I looked for my soul, but my soul I could not see.
I looked for my God, but my God eluded me.
I looked for a friend, and then I found all three.
—THOMAS BLAKE

I treated him; God cured him.
—AMBROISE PARE

I asked God for strength, and He gave me problems.
—FRED KOEHLER

I stand before this crucifix every time I put on my white
leather. I'm not really religious-I don't go to church-
but I believe in God. I'm God-fearing. Why, I don't know.
—EVEL KNIEVEL

It is the orderliness of the whole universe about us—
from the smallest atomic structure to the most enormous
thing we can imagine; galaxies millions of light years
across, all traveling in prescribed orbits in relation to one
another—that shows me there is a God.
—JOHN GLENN

I have no one, but I stand with God.
—TAWAKALITU

If a man cannot sing as he carries his cross, he had better
drop it.
—HAVELOCK ELLIS

I had never been truly in solitary confinement; God's
companionship does not stop at the door of a jail cell.
—MARTIN LUTHER KING, JR.

I asked God for all things that I might enjoy life. He gave
me life—that I might enjoy all things.
FROM AN OLD CONFERERATE PRAYER BOOK

I've studied so many religions to get to the spot where I
am now. I've studied metaphysics and Krishnaism. To me,
Albert Schweitzer is religion. I'm everything. You're everything. We're all one. We're all one with the universe-
with God.
—DORIS DAY

170

Jesus did not try to get the people out of the slums; He tried to get the slums out of the people.
—PAUL HARVEY

Just as there comes a warm sunbeam into every cottage window, so comes a love-beam of God's care and pity for every separate need.
—NATHANIEL HAWTHORNE

Live each day at a time, and with the assurance that God can be depended upon to carry you through the future as He has in the past.
—MARY THOMPSON

Let each man think himself an act of God.
—BAILEY

Lord, through this Hour be Thou our guide; so, by Thy power No foot shall slide.
—WESTMINSTER CHIME

Let us not pray for lighter burdens but for stronger backs.
—ROGER BABSON

Living right is thinking unnegatively. I want my life to say, "She learned what love, life, and truth are about. She loved God."
—GINGER ROGERS

Let us not be frightened by the problems that confront us, but rather give Thee thanks that Thou has matched us with this hour. May we resolve, God helping us, to be part of the answer and not the part of the problem.
—PETER MARSHALL
(from a prayer given before the Senate when he was Chaplain)

May the warm winds of Heaven blow softly on this house and may the Great Spirit bless all who enter here.
—THE CHEROKEE PRAYER

Mortal I know I am, short-lived; and yet, whenever I watch the multitude of swirling stars, then I no longer tread this earth, but rise to feast with God, and enjoy the food of the immortals.
—PTOLEMY

My country is the world and my religion is to do good.
—THOMAS PAINE

Memory enables man to play God.
—HAL BOYLE

More things are wrought by prayer than this world dreams of.
—WILLIAM SHAKESPEARE

May God bless you all on your journey to the stars.
—LADYBIRD JOHNSON

No one is without sin, but somehow God works through imperfect lives to fulfill His purpose.
—REV. ROBERT RYDELL

Nature is a revelation of God; Art is a revelation of man.
—HENRY WADSWORTH LONGFELLOW

Oh, Lord, Thy ocean is so large,
And my boat is so small.
—OFTEN QUOTED BY JACK KENNEDY

Oh, Lord, give to the hungry, food; And give to the well-fed, a hunger for justice.
—DAVID FROST
      (a South American prayer)

Oh, Lord, don't let nothin' happen that You and me can't handle together.
—AN OLD NEGRO PRAYER

172

Pray to be stronger men! Do not pray for tasks equal to your powers. Pray for powers equal to your tasks.
—PHILLIPS BROOKS

Religion is a great force—and the only real motive force in the world; but you must get at a man through his own religion, not through yours.
—GEORGE BERNARD SHAW

Someday scientists will turn their laboratories over to the study of God and prayer, and the spiritual forces which, as yet, have hardly been scratched.
—CHARLES STEINMETZ

To reach the port of Heaven, we must sail sometimes with the wind, and sometimes against it. But we must sail, and not drift or lie at anchor.
—OLIVER WENDELL HOLMES

The difficulty is that our concept of God is too small. God is infinite—infinite in His wisdom, goodness and love.
—WILLIAM L. POWERS.

The human mind cannot comprehend the greatness of God.
—C. CORCOS

'Tis wise to learn; 'tis God-like to create.
—JOHN SAXE

The only religious way to think of death is as part and parcel of life; to regard it, with the understanding and the emotions, as the inviolable condition of life.
—THOMAS MANN

Thank God every morning when you get up that you have something that must be done, whether you like it or not.
—CHARLES KINGSLEY

The Old Testament Bible stories have been the warp and woof of my life—helping me to understand the New Testament,

173

v it affects my own life.
JOEL HARPER

believe in God is to yearn for His existence, and, furthermore, it is to act as if He did exist.
–MIGUEL DE UNAMUNO

To a man with an empty stomach, food is God.
–MOHANDAS GANDHI

Toleration is the best religion.
–VICTOR HUGO

The universe is centered on neither the earth nor the sun. It is centered on God.
–ALFRED NOYES

'Tis God gives skill, but not without man's hands: He could not make Antonio Stradivari's violins without Antonio.
–GEORGE ELIOT

The Lord don't put no more on you than you can stand.
–JOAN LITTLE

The best way to know God is to love many things.
–VINCENT VAN GOGH

To cultivate a garden is to walk with God.
–CHRISTIAN BOVEE

'Tis Heaven alone that is given away;
'Tis only God may be had for the asking.
–JAMES RUSSELL LOWELL

Who rises from prayer a better man, his prayer is answered.
–GEORGE MEREDITH

Whatever you do, put your whole heart and soul into it, as into work done for God.
–ST. PAUL

What matters to so many men-to you, perhaps, is what

their friends think of them—what their people think, what all the people in all the streets in every town and village think. It is so much easier to be responsible only to God.
—R. C. HUTCHINSON

When men in a ship pull on a rope fastened to an anchor, they do not pull the anchor toward them but themselves toward the anchor. In the same way, when we pray, our words are not to pull God toward us, but to pull us toward Him.
—CLEMENT OF ALEXANDRIA

When I heard the church bells ring, I thought I heard the voice of God.
—ALBERT SCHWEITZER

What is religion? That which is never spoken.
—HENRY DAVID THOREAU

When I was a young lad, my Sunday school teacher mentioned rather casually one day that she could never stand seeing any books placed on top of the Bible. I can't either. Her philosophy has staid with me a lifetime.
—HOWARD HARRIS

You can't measure God in scientific terms. You can't see, feel, smell or touch religious power. It is intangible. But if we let Christian principles guide our lives, our senses don't have to pick them up. We see the results of this guiding power in our lives and in the lives of others. We know it is there.
—JOHN GLENN

You don't make religion work. You let it work.
—LLOYD C. DOUGLAS

You've gut to git up airly
Ef you want to take in God.
—JAMES RUSSEL LOWELL

Whatever be our station, with Providence fer guide,
Such fine circumstances ort to make us satisfied;
Fer the world is full of roses, and the roses full of dew
And the dew is full of Heavenly love,
That drips fer me and you.
—JAMES WHITCOMB RILEY

What does the Lord require of thee, but to do justly, and
to love mercy, and to walk humbly with thy God.
—THE BIBLE
           MICAH 6:8

NUGGETS

A boy's will is the wind's will,
And the thoughts of youth are long, long thoughts.
—HENRY WADSWORTH LONGFELLOW

Any man's death diminishes me, because I am involved in
mankind, and therefore never send to know for whom the bell
tolls; it tolls for thee.
—JOHN DONNE

And Virtue, though in rags, will keep me warm.
—JOHN DRYDEN

Away from the world with its toils and its cares,
I've a snug little kingdom up four pair of stairs.
—WILLIAM THACKERAY

A little learning is a dangerous thing;
Drink deep, or taste not the Pierian Spring.
—ALEXANDER POPE

As I would not be a slave, so I would not be a master.
—ABRAHAM LINCOLN

A man is rich in proportion to the number of things which
he can afford to leave alone.
—HENRY DAVID THOREAU

And sweet is death who puts an end to pain.
—ALFRED TENNYSON

And he looks the whole world in the face,
For he owes not any man.
—HENRY WADSWORTH LONGFELLOW

A little kingdom I possess, where thoughts and feelings
dwell; And very hard the task I find of governing it well.
—LOUISA MAY ALCOTT

Absence of occupation is not rest,
A mind quite vacant is a mind distress'd.
—WILLIAM COWPER

179

All who joy   would win must share it—
Happiness was born a twin.
—LORD BYRON

And in the world, as in the school,
I'd say, how fate may change and shift;
The prize be sometimes with the fool,
The race not always to the swift.
—WILLIAM THACKERAY

A thing of beauty is a joy forever.
—JOHN KEATS

All the world's a stage, and all the men and women merely
players; they have their exits and their entrances, and one
man in his time plays many parts.
—WILLIAM SHAKESPEARE

And the night shall be filled with music,
And the cares that infest the day,
Shall fold their tents, like the Arabs,
And as silently steal away.
—HENRY WADSWORTH LONGFELLOW

Again I saw, again I heard
The rolling river, the morning bird.
Beauty through my senses stole;
I yielded myself to the perfect whole.
—RALPH WALDO EMERSON

But, Friend, to me—
He is all fault who hath no fault at all.
For who loves me must have a touch of earth.
—ALFRED TENNYSON

Be glad, and your friends are many;
Be sad, and you lose them all,
—ELLA WHEELER WILCOX

Breathes there the man, with soul so dead,

Who never to himself hath said,
This is my own, my native land!
—SIR WALTER SCOTT

Ah! that thou couldst know the joy,
Ere it passes, barefoot boy!
—JOHN GREENLEAF WHITTIER

Be not the first by whom the new are tried
Nor yet the last to lay the old aside.
—ALEXANDER POPE

Be strong! We are not here to play, to dream, to drift
We have hard work to do, and loads to lift;
Shun not the struggle—face it; 'tis God's gift.
—MALTBIE D. BABCOCK

But he that filches from me my good name,
Robs me of that which not enriches him,
And makes me poor indeed.
—WILLIAM SHAKESPEARE

Better by far you should forget and smile—
Than that you should remember and be sad.
—CHRISTINA ROSSETTI

Be good, sweet maid, and let who will be clever;
Do noble things, not dream them all day long;
And so make Life, Death, and that For Ever
One grand sweet song.
—CHARLES KINGSLEY

But pleasures are like poppies spread—
You seize the flow'r, its bloom is shed;
Or like the snow falls in the river—
A moment white—then melts forever.
—ROBERT BURNS

Blessed is he who has found his work;
Let him ask no other blessedness.
—THOMAS CARLYLE

181

But I've a rendezvous with Death
At midnight in some flaming town,
When Spring trips north again this year,
And I to my pledged word am true,
I shall not fail that rendezvous.
—ALAN SEEGER

Come, my friends, 'Tis not too late
To seek a newer world. . . .
To strive, to seek, to find, and not to yield.
—ALFRED TENNYSON

Consistency is the hobgoblin of small minds.
—RALPH WALDO EMERSON

Come forth into the light of things,
Let Nature be your teacher.
—WILLIAM WORDSWORTH

Come down from your shelves, ye tried and true!
O wise and good of the elder day!
For I'm always at home, my friends, to you,
And you're always welcome to say your say!
—R. W. WADDY

Don't say things. What you are stands over you the while,
and thunders so that I cannot hear what you say to the con -
trary.
—RALPH WALDO EMERSON

Dost thou love life? Then do not squander Time;
For that's the stuff Life is made of.
—BENJAMIN FRANKLIN

Death comes with a crawl, or comes with a pounce,
And whether he's slow or spry,
It isn't the fact that you're dead that counts,
But only, how did you die?
—EDMUND VANCE COOKE

Exult, O shores, and ring, O bells!
But I, with mournful tread,
Walk the deck my Captain lies,
Fallen cold and dead.
—WALT WHITMAN

Every man carries with him the world in which he must
live.
—F. MARION CRAWFORD

For some must watch while some must sleep;
Thus runs the world away.
—WILLIAM SHAKESPEARE

From the little spark may burst a mighty flame.
—ALIGHIERI DANTE

For life is the mirror of king and slave,
'Tis just what we are and do;
Then give to the world the best you have
And the best will come back to you.
—MADELINE S. BRIDGES

Fie, what a spendthrift is he of his tongue.
—WILLIAM SHAKESPEARE

For fools rush in where angels fear to tread.
—ALEXANDER POPE

For of all sad words of tongue or pen,
The saddest are these: It might have been.
—JOHN GREENLEAF WHITTIER

Grow old with me!
The best is yet to be.
—ROBERT BROWNING

Give every man thine ear, but few thy voice.
—WILLIAM SHAKESPEARE

Happy the man, and happy he alone,
He who can call today his own.
—JOHN DRYDEN

How does the meadow flower its bloom unfold?
Because the lovely little flower is free—
Down to its root, and, in that freedom, bold.
—WILLIAM WORDSWORTH

Hope springs eternal in the human breast.
—ALEXANDER POPE

How poor are they, that have not patience!
What wound did ever heal, but by degrees?
—WILLIAM SHAKESPEARE

He gained a world; he gave that world
Its grandest lesson: On, sail on!
—JOAQUIN MILLER

He makes no friend who never made a foe.
—ALFRED TENNYSON

His life was gentle, and the elements
So mix'd in him that Nature might stand up.
And say to all the world, "This was a man!"
—WILLIAM SHAKESPEARE

Heap on more wood! The wind is chill;
But let it whistle as it will,
We'll keep our Christmas merry still.
—SIR WALTER SCOTT

How happy is he born or taught,
That serveth not another's will;
Whose armour is his honest thought,
And simple truth his utmost skill!
—SIR HENRY WOTTON

He jests at scars, that never felt a wound.
—WILLIAM SHAKESPEARE

Here he lies where he longed to be;
Home is the sailor, home from the sea,
And the hunter home from the hill.
—ROBERT LOUIS STEVENSON

How sweet, how passing sweet, is solitude!
But grant me still a friend in my retreat
Whom I may whisper—solitude is sweet.
—WILLIAM COWPER

He lives to learn, in life's hard school,
How few who pass above him,
Lament their triumph and his loss,
Like her, because they love him.
—JOHN GREENLEAF WHITTIER

How far that little candle throws his beam!
So shines a good deed in a naughty world.
—WILLIAM SHAKESPEARE

He gives only the worthless gold
Who gives from a sense of duty.
—JAMES RUSSELL LOWELL

Hitch your wagon to a star.
—RALPH WALDO EMERSON

I must be measured by my soul;
The mind's the standard of the man.
—ISAAC WATTS

In all the silent manliness of grief.
—OLIVER GOLDSMITH

I disapprove of what you say, but I will defend to the

185

death your right to say it.
—VOLTAIRE

It matters not how long we live, but how.
—PHILIP JAMES BAILEY

I envy nobody, no, not I
And nobody envies me.
—CHARLES MACKAY

If you want to be happy, be.
—ALEXEI TOLSTOI

I live not in myself, but I become Portion of that around
me.
—LORD BYRON

If you strike a thorn or rose, keep a goin',
If it hails or if it snows, keep a goin'.
—FRANK LEBBY STANTON

I wasted time, and now doth time waste me.
—WILLIAM SHAKESPEARE

If you can talk with crowds and keep your virtue,
Or walk with Kings—nor lose the common touch.
—RUDYARD KIPLING

I pray thee, then,
Write me as one that loves his fellow men.
—LEIGH HUNT

If I can stop one heart from breaking
I shall not live in vain.
—EMILY DICKINSON

I do not know what I was playing,
Or what I was dreaming then;
But I struck one chord of music,

Like the sound of a great Amen.
—ADELAIDE ANNE PROCTER

I'm a part of all that I have met;
Yet all experience is an arch whereth.
Gleams that untravel'd world.
—ALFRED TENNYSON

I want, by understanding myself, to unde
—KATHERINE MANSFIELD

It is a wise father that knows his own child.
—WILLIAM SHAKESPEARE

I cannot say, and I will not say
That he is dead. He is just away!
—JAMES WHITCOMB RILEY

It takes a heap o' livin' in a house t' make it home.
—EDGAR A. GUEST

I never found the companion that was so companionable
as solitude.
—HENRY DAVID THOREAU

Into each life some rain must fall,
Some days must be dark and dreary.
—HENRY WADSWORTH LONGFELLOW

I just hit him with a great big hunk of silence.
—JAMES WHITCOMB RILEY

I think that I shall never see
A poem lovely as a tree.
—JOYCE KILMER

In this world there are only two tragedies. One is not getting what one wants; and the other is getting it.
—OSCAR WILDE

saw a Moor—I never saw the sea.
now I how the Heather looks
and what a Billow be.
—EMILY DICKINSON

Is it so small a thing
To have enjoyed the sun,
To have lived light in the spring,
To have loved, To have thought, To have done?
—MATTHEW ARNOLD

I keep six honest serving men;
(They taught me all I knew):
Their names are What and Why and When
And How and Where and Who.
—RUDYARD KIPLING

I am only one,
But still I am one.
—EDWARD EVERETT HALE

It matters not how strait the gate,
How charged with punishments the scroll,
I am the master of my fate;
I am the captain of my soul.
—WILLIAM ERNEST HENLEY

I'll speak to thee in silence.
—WILLIAM SHAKESPEARE

I am monarch of all I survey,
My right there is none to dispute.
—WILLIAM COWPER

It is not raining rain to me,
It's raining daffodils;
In every dimpled drop I see,
Wildflowers on the hills.
—ROBERT LOVEMAN

I have learned silence from the talkative.
—KAHIL GIBRAN

If a man does not keep pace with his companions, perhaps
it is because he hears a different drummer. Let him step
to the music which he hears, however measured or far away.
—HENRY DAVID THOREAU

Just to be good—That is enough—enough!
—JAMES WHITCOMB RILEY

Knowledge comes, but wisdom lingers.
—ALFRED TENNYSON

Lost, yesterday, somewhere between sunrise and sunset,
two golden hours, set with sixty diamond minutes. No reward offered for they are lost forever.
—HORACE MANN

Laugh, and the world laughs with you;
Weep, and you weep alone.
—ELLA WHEELER WILCOX

Love your life, poor as it is. You may perhaps have some
pleasant, thrilling, glorious hours, even in a poorhouse.
—HENRY DAVID THOREAU

Let there be spaces in your togetherness.
—KAHIL GIBRAN

Lives of great men all remind us
We can make our lives sublime.
—HENRY WADSWORTH LONGFELLOW

Let me live in my house by the side of the road
And be a friend of man.
—SAM WALTER FOSS

Learn the sweet magic of a cheerful face;

Not always smiling, but at least serene.
—OLIVER WENDELL HOLMES

Love looks not with the eyes but with the mind.
—WILLIAM SHAKESPEARE

Let's go a visitin' back to Griggsby' Station—
Back where we ust to be so happy and so pore!
—JAMES WHITCOMB RILEY

Life is real! Life is earnest!
And the grave is not its goal.
—HENRY WADSWORTH LONGFELLOW

Lord of himself, though not of lands;
And having nothing, yet hath all.
—SIR HENRY WOTTON

Like as the waves make toward the pebbled shore,
So do our minutes hasten to their end.
—WILLIAM SHAKESPEARE

My candle burns at both ends;
It will not last the night;
But, ah, my foes, and oh, my friends—
It gives a lovely light.
—EDNA ST. VINCENT MILLAY

'Mid pleasures and palaces though we may roam,
Be it ever so humble, there's no place like home.
—JOHN HOWARD PAYNE

May you live all the days of your life.
—JOATHAN SWIFT

My very chains and I grew friends,
So much a long communion tends
To make us what we are: even I
Regain'd my freedom with a sigh.
—LORD BYRON

Most folks are about as happy as they make up their minds to be.
—ABRAHAM LINCOLN

My heart leaps up when I behold a rainbow in the sky.
—WILLIAM WORDSWORTH

Not what we give, but what we share,
For the gift without the giver is bare.
—JAMES RUSSELL LOWELL

Neither a borrower, nor a lender be;
For loan oft loses both itself and friend.
—WILLIAM SHAKESPEARE

No man is an Island, entire of itself;
every man is a piece of the Continent, a part of the main.
—JOHN DONNE

Nothing is so much to be feared as fear.
—HENRY DAVID THOREAU

No man is useless while he has a friend.
—ROBERT LOUIS STEVENSON

Nothing that is can pause or stay;
The moon will wax, the moon will wane,
The mist and cloud will turn to rain,
The rain to mist and cloud again,
Tomorrow be today.
—HENRY WADSWORTH LONGFELLOW

No man can lose what he never had.
—IZAAK WALTON

Oh, what a tangled web we weave,
When first we practice to deceive!
—SIR WALTER SCOTT

Ort a mortul be complainin' when dumb animals rejoice?
—JAMES WHITCOMB RILEY

One ship drives east and another drives west
By the selfsame winds that blow,
'Tis the set of sails and not the gales
Which tells us the way to go.
—ELLA WHEELER WILCOX

Oh why should the spirit of mortal be proud?
—WILLIAM KNOX

Oh, a trouble's a ton, or a trouble's an ounce,
Or a trouble is what you make it.
—EDMUND VANCE COOKE

O the old trundle-bed where I slept when a boy!
What canopied king might not covet the joy?
—JAMES WHITCOMB RILEY

One hour of life, crowded to the full with glorious action,
and filled with noble risks, is worth whole years of those
mean observances of paltry decorum.
—SIR WALTER SCOTT

O wad some power the giftie gie us
To see oursels as others see us!
—ROBERT BURNS

Out of the night that covers me,
Black as the Pit from pole to pole,
I thank whatever gods may be
For my unconquerable soul.
—WILLIAM ERNEST HENLEY

O God, give us serenity to accept what cannot be changed,
courage to change what should be changed, and wisdom to
distinguish the one from the other.
—REINHOLD NIEBUHR

Our life is frittered away by detail. . . . Simplify, simplify.
—HENRY DAVID THOREAU

Oh leave this barren spot to me!
Spare, woodman, spare the beechen tree!
—THOMAS CAMPBELL

Procrastination is the thief of time.
Year after year it steals, till all are fled,
And to the mercies of a moment leaves
The vast concerns of an eternal scene.
—EDWARD YOUNG

Roll on, thou deep and dark blue ocean—roll!
Ten thousand fleets sweep over thee in vain;
Man marks the earth with ruin—
His control stops with the shore.
—LORD BYRON

Reflect on your present blessings, of which every man
has many—not on your past misfortunes, of which all men
have some.
—CHARLES DICKENS

Short words are best and the old words when short are
best of all.
—SIR WINSTON CHURCHILL

Silence is the perfectest herald of joy;
I were but little happy, if I could say how much.
—WILLIAM SHAKESPEARE

Something attempted, something done,
Has earned a night's repose.
—HENRY WADSWORTH LONGFELLOW

Stone walls do not a prison make, nor iron bars a cage.
—RICHARD LOVELACE

So live, that when thy summons comes to join the innumerable caravan which moves to that mysterious realm where each shall take his chamber in the silent halls of death—
Thou go not, like the quarry-slave at night, but, like one that wraps the drapery of his couch about him, and lies down to pleasant dreams.
—WILLIAM CULLEN BRYANT

Self is the only prison that can ever bind the soul.
—HENRY VAN DYKE

Some go to conquer things; some go to try them;
Some go to dream then, And some go to bed!
—JAMES WHITCOMB RILEY

Sweet are the uses of adversity.
Which, like the toad, ugly and venemous,
Wears yet a precious jewel in his head.
—WILLIAM SHAKESPEARE

Ships that pass in the night, and speak each other in passing—
So on the ocean of life we pass and speak one another,
Only a look and a voice; then darkness again and a silence.
—HENRY WADSWORTH LONGFELLOW

Time you old gypsy man,
Will you not stay.
Put up your caravan
Just for one day.
—RALPH HODGSON

The more things change, the more they remain the same.
—ALPHONSE KARR

Talk happiness. The world is sad enough without your woe.
—ELLA WHEELER WILCOX

To me every hour of the light and dark is a miracle;
Every cubic inch of space is a miracle.
—WALT WHITMAN

There is nothing either good or bad, but thinking makes
it so.
—WILLIAM SHAKESPEARE

'Tis strange—but true; for truth is always strange;
Stranger than fiction.
—LORD BYRON

They also serve who only stand and wait.
—JOHN MILTON

This is the forest primeval,
The murmuring pines and the hemlocks. . .
Bearded with moss, and in garments green,
Indistinct in the twilight,
Stand like Druids of old, with voices sad and prophetic.
—HENRY WADSWORTH LONGFELLOW

The best laid schemes O' mice and men
Gang aft a-gley.
—ROBERT BURNS

There's a divinity that shapes our ends,
Rough-hew them how we will.
—WILLIAM SHAKESPEARE

The more we love our friends, the less we flatter them;
it is by excusing nothing that pure love shows itself.
—MOLIERE

To err is human, to forgive divine.
—ALEXANDER POPE

There is a pleasure in the pathless woods,

195

There is a rapture on the lonely shore;
I love not man the less, but Nature more.
—LORD BYRON

The friends thou hast, and their adoption tried,
Grapple them to thy soul with hoops of steel.
—WILLIAM SHAKESPEARE

The world is too much with us; late and soon,
Getting and spending, we lay waste our powers;
Little we see in Nature that is ours.
—WILLIAM WORDSWORTH

Turn, turn, my wheel, all things must change,
To something new, to something strange.
—HENRY WADSWORTH LONGFELLOW

The swiftest traveler is he that goes afoot.
—HENRY DAVID THOREAU

There is something in a face,
An air, and a peculiar grace,
Which boldest painters cannot trace.
—WILLIAM SOMERVILLE

'Tis better to have loved and lost
Than never to have loved at all.
—ALFRED TENNYSON

"The time has come," the Walrus said,
"To talk of many things;
Of shoes and ships and sealing-wax—
Of Cabbages and kings."
—LEWIS CARROLL

There is a destiny that makes us brothers;
None goes his way alone;
All that we send into the lives of others
Comes back into our own.
—EDWIN MARKHAM

196

The curfew tolls the knell of parting day,
The lowing herd winds slowly o'er the lea,
The plowman homeward plods his weary way,
And leaves the world to darkness and to me.
—THOMAS GRAY

Then the little Hiawatha learned of every bird its language,
Learned their names and all their secrets.
—HENRY WADSWORTH LONGFELLOW

The fault, dear Brutus, is not in our stars
But in ourselves, that we are underlings.
—WILLIAM SHAKESPEARE

Though nothing can bring back the hour
Of splendor in the grass, of glory in the flower.
—WILLIAM WORDSWORTH

The supreme happiness of life is the conviction that we
are loved.
—VICTOR HUGO

The quality of mercy is not strain'd,
It droppeth as the gentle rain from Heaven
Upon the place beneath:
It is twice bless'd; It blesseth him that gives and him that takes.
—WILLIAM SHAKESPEARE

Turn back the leaves of life. Don't read the story.
Let's find the pictures, and fancy all the rest.
—JAMES WHITCOMB RILEY

That man is the richest whose pleasures are the cheapest.
—HENRY DAVID THOREAU

Though the mills of God grind slowly,
yet they grind exceeding small.
—FRIEDRICH VON LOGAU

Tongues in trees, books in the running brooks,
Sermons in stones, and good in everything.
—WILLIAM SHAKESPEARE

The mind is its own place, and in itself
Can make a heav'n of hell, a hell of heav'n.
—JOHN MILTON

There comes an hour of sadness with the setting of the sun,
Not for the sins committed, but the things I have not done.
—MINOT JUDSON SAVAGE

To live in hearts we leave behind is not to die.
—THOMAS CAMPBELL

There is a little good and a little bad in every living thing;
The bee makes wax and honey, but oh, how he can sting!
—ROBERT LOUIS STEVENSON

Though my soul may set in darkness
It will rise in perfect light;
I have loved the stars too fondly
To be fearful of the night.
—SARAH WILLIAMS

There is a tide in the affairs of men, which, taken at the
flood, leads on to fortune.
—WILLIAM SHAKESPEARE

To be what we are and to become what we are capable of
becoming, is the only end of life.
—ROBERT LOUIS STEVENSON

' 'Tis distance lends enchantment to the view,
And robes the mountain in its azure hue.
—THOMAS CAMPBELL

The world is so full of a number of things,
I'm sure we should all be as happy as kings.
—ROBERT LOUIS STEVENSON

The setting sun is reflected from the windows of the
almshouse as brightly as from the rich man's abode.
—HENRY DAVID THOREAU

The heights by great men reached and kept
Were not attained by sudden flight;
But they, while their companions slept
Were toiling upward in the night.
—HENRY WADSWORTH LONGFELLOW

The great purpose of life is to live it.
—OLIVER WENDELL HOLMES

There is no vice so simple but assumes
Some mark of virtue on his outward parts.
—WILLIAM SHAKESPEARE

Under the wide and starry sky,
Dig the grave and let me lie;
Glad did I live and gladly die,
And I laid me down with a will.
—ROBERT LOUIS STEVENSON

What in me is dark
Illumine,
What is low raise and support.
—JOHN MILTON

Where there is sorrow there is holy ground.
—OSCAR WILDE

We do pray for mercy,
And that same prayer doth teach us all

To render the deeds of mercy.
—WILLIAM SHAKESPEARE

When I remember all the friends so linked together
I've seen around me fall, like leaves in wintry weather,
I feel like one who treads alone
Some banquet-hall deserted.
—THOMAS MOORE

Yet it isn't the gold that I'm wanting
So much as just finding the gold.
—ROBERT W. SERVICE

Youth, what man's age is like to be doth show,
We may our ends by our beginnings know.
—SIR JOHN DENHAM

Yet I doubt not through the ages
One increasing purpose runs,
And the thoughts of men are widened
With the process of the suns.
—ALFRED TENNYSON

You have no enemies, you say?
Alas, my friend, the boast is poor,
He who has mingled in the fray
Must have made foes.
—CHARLES MACKAY

You never know what life means till you die;
Even throughout life, 'tis death that makes life live,
Gives it whatever the significance.
—ROBERT BROWNING

All your strength is in your union,
All your danger is in discord;
Therefore be at peace henceforward,

And as brothers live together.
—HENRY WADSWORTH LONGFELLOW

Beauty is in the eye of the beholder.
—MARGARET WOLFE HUNGERFORD

The old poets little knew
What comfort they could be to man.
—SARAH ORNE JEWETT

His brow is wet with honest sweat,
He earns whate'er he can,
And looks the whole world in the face
For he owes not any man.
—HENRY WADSWORTH LONGFELLOW

This above all: to thine own self be true,
And it must follow, as the night the day,
Thou canst not then be false to any man.
—WILLIAM SHAKESPEARE

Thus conscience does make cowards of us all.
—WILLIAM SHAKESPEARE

Where ignorance is bliss,
'Tis folly to be wise.
—THOMAS GRAY

We'll tak a cup o' kindness yet
For auld lang syne!
—ROBERT BURNS